Learning Hov   lf
and Your Fut   e

DISCOVER

LF

THROUGH

PALM

READING

By

Rita Robinson

NEW PAGE BOOKS
A division of The Career Press, Inc.
Franklin Lakes, NJ

DISCOVER YOURSELF THROUGH PALM READING
EDITED BY JODI BRANDON
TYPESET BY EILEEN DOW MUNSON
Cover design by DesignConcept
Printed in the U.S.A. by Book-mart Press

To order this title, please call toll-free 1-800-CAREER-1 (NJ and Canada: 201-848-0310) to order using VISA or MasterCard, or for further information on books from Career Press.

The Career Press, Inc., 3 Tice Road, PO Box 687,
Franklin Lakes, NJ 07417
www.careerpress.com
www.newpagebooks.com

Library of Congress Cataloging-in-Publication Data

Robinson, Rita
    Discover yourself through palm reading : learning how to read yourself and your future, line by line / by Rita Robinson.
        p. cm.
    Includes bibliographical references and index.
    ISBN 1-56414-542-5 (pbk.)
    1. Palmistry. I. Title.

BF921 .R625 2001
133.6—dc21

2001031541

For Linda Liebman,
years of ongoing discovery.

ACKNOWLEDGMENTS

Many thanks to the countless numbers of people of all ages, ethnic groups, political persuasions, from rich and struggling to gnarly and gentle, who have shared their hands with me so that I might become more aware, open, knowledgeable, and curious about the art of palm reading.

Special thanks to Doreen Baylus and Dana Brookins for undergoing the ink blot test and still considering me a friend. Special thanks, also, to my editor Jodi Brandon, who nudged me for a few more needed explanations and clarifications and to Barbara Cunningham-McEwen for her thoughtful graphics.

ONTENTS

INTRODUCTION

"No," is my immediate response when someone asks if I believe in fate because I practice palm reading. The hands provide clues to talents, capabilities, personalities, temperaments, desires, weaknesses, and strengths, rather than offer a path in life that must be followed. Once individuals are aware of what they're about, they're more free to make their own choices and decisions—and to take responsibility for them. A choice made at a certain point in life leads to another choice down the road. Sometimes wrong decisions are made, or maybe we fail at something. Life is also about learning from our failures. After all, as Thomas A. Edison said, "I have not failed 10,000 times. I have successfully found 10,000 ways that will not work."

But we may learn just as much from our successes. Edison, by all accounts, ended up very successful. So life is not fated, although there are some things for which we may not have control, such as certain illnesses (although some might be averted or minimized with lifestyle changes), wars, pestilence, the weather, and where and to whom we're born.

Palmistry serves as a guide: a way to gain insight into what is going on in our lives and what outcomes might be possible. Any number of questions can be answered by studying the palm, but the answers are fluid, providing several choices.

This is as true for palmistry as it originally was when the ancients studied astrology, cast runes, or paid attention to other signs that served as guides for self-discovery. The reading itself does not answer the questions. Individuals choose from the different options offered and become active participants in their own destiny.

Perhaps a woman who has dedicated the first portion of her life to raising children discovers in mid-life a desire to counsel others, coupled with artistic ability. Her hand might show a few years ahead of time that she is going to return to school. Her goal might be a degree in art therapy. Once the original idea (that she's going to return to school) is implanted in the consciousness, the more likely the idea will manifest itself.

Maybe a man has dreamed of escaping the confines of an office in exchange for the outdoors, and the hand shows that a major change in his work will occur in his late 40s. The palmist may notice that a few years of struggle will be necessary to make the transition. Often, it's been in the man's subconscious all along, waiting for the right nudge to bring it into the open. Again, it becomes a matter of choice. The information is there for the man to ponder. Will he want to tolerate the years of struggle, akin to starting over again? Only he can make that decision.

Questions about a person's career rank at the top of the most frequently asked, but "Will I have a long life?" is still number one. People believe that the length of the line of life predicts how long they will live. It does not. But it does provide clues about a person's energy level and how he or she approaches life. The line may show the approximate ages at which energy is dissipated or when it bursts forth with new ideas and growth. Joined with other markings on the hand, it tells stories of possible job changes, new endeavors, perhaps a return to school, illness, disappointments, and rewards.

Palmistry is not just about how long we will live, how many lovers we will have, or how rich we'll be. It speaks to the quality of our lives—what we're truly capable of doing and being. Whether or not we act on those capabilities is a choice. The answers to those questions may be by-products (and shown by markings on the hand) of our journey through life.

There are no bad hands, although some of the classic palmistry books show the biases of the culture in which they were written. European cultures favored the long, slender hand and fingers, so those became top dog in books written by them prior to the 20th century, because they were geared to the nobility. Palmistry was a favorite at court. Never mind that half the world was living in cold, frigid climates that traditionally bore hands with shorter fingers in order to conserve body heat.

More subtle distinctions also exist. Say a certain marking, pattern, or shape indicates that a person likes the center of attention, enjoys a good argument, is shy, or is nosy, traits that could be seen as undesirable in some cultures, or by some people. But under different circumstances they are as important as being assertive, being a positive thinker, or minding our own business. It takes those who enjoy the center of attention to be an actor or a politician; if everyone minded his or her own business, someone who is mistreating a child might not be turned in to the proper authorities. In other words, nearly every trait can be of use in society. So, once we understand our quirks and idiosyncrasies, they can be seen as useful and positive rather than negative. And we can see the idiosyncrasies of others in a lighter vein.

We can move beyond the constraints we often place on ourselves when we believe that we must conform to this or that dictate, which makes us miserable. Obviously a certain amount of conformity is needed to function in a society, which is why we have laws, as well as rituals and cultural taboos. But these needn't squash an individual's personal likes, dislikes, goals, and beliefs. After reading hands for 30 years, I've found that people are far more capable, adaptable, wise, and creative than they think themselves to be, or as others might see them. A friend, a psychotherapist and former Jesuit priest, who was a practicing Buddhist and Catholic, liked to think of people as rough-cut diamonds who become more polished as they travel life's journey. Palmistry allows us to encourage the polishing.

We're actually pretty tough. Studies of people older than 85 at the University of California, San Francisco, show that when they were younger, some had survived cancer and other catastrophic diseases, lost children and other loved ones, and yet most were upbeat, even if debilitated. Other studies at Purdue University of the oldest of the old showed the same thing. Their attitudes, plus genetics and plain old luck, all count toward a successful journey at any age. And that's a major part of what can be discovered by studying the hand.

Too often in reading palms, we observe people who are unhappy in their work, play, love, friendships, and spiritual lives. By studying the hand, we can use findings as guides to understanding our own natures, as well as the nature of others, and move forward toward a deeper understanding of our place in the universe.

We learn why some of us are risk-takers in work, maybe preferring to be self-employed, while others choose to work for a large corporation.

Some people prefer isolation to crowds, and others enjoy the company of others more readily than being by themselves. A person may discover that he or she has writing abilities, is really better at math than once believed, or has leadership characteristics never before tapped. We're all unique. How boring it would be otherwise.

One couple whose hands I read co-own a florist business. They acknowledge that she is best at the business end of their work and in triggering new ideas; he is the more gregarious, hands-on type. She supplies the ideas and he implements them. Together their business thrives, because they are aware of their strengths and weaknesses.

Each inborn and acquired characteristic manifests itself differently as shown by the shapes of the hands and fingers, the color of the palms and accompanying lines, and the placement of lines and mounts.

Even the way we hold our hands offers clues into our personalities, because the position registers on the brain.

Neuroscientists at the University of California, Los Angeles found, through nuclear magnetic resonance imagery, that regions of the brain are highlighted when the fingers become active and that those same regions also become active when a person imagines the same action of the fingers without actually moving them. We are, indeed, as we think.

Also, brain development remains greatly malleable throughout childhood and, given stimulation and enrichment through lifetime learning, can repeatedly blossom anew as we age. Other studies show that adults in their 60s and 70s grow new brain cells, whereas it was previously thought those cells stopped renewing at a certain age.

Another branch of science (genetics) offers validation that humans inherit a good portion of what we are about. Some of those inherited characteristics show in the hand. Some scientists believe that at least 50 percent of our personality and certain characteristics are genetic. Attitude, coping skills, energy, attributes, physical and mental strengths, and likes and dislikes all play roles in how we operate in this world. Yet our life patterns and choices are not set in cement, because we are all capable of making the most of our inherent characteristics and also of making changes. Along with that, some scientists believe that cultural expectations play a large part in our development, our ability to change, and our resilience to cope with adversity.

To get the most from palmistry it's necessary to understand a great many different markings, because one line or one particular shape tells little by itself. A line might need to be read in light of the way the thumbs bend or in combination with another line. In other words, no one manifestation tells the complete story. The hand must be read holistically. Therefore, this book deals first with the basics of palmistry and then how to apply what has been learned to everyday life.

Palmistry is fun. Life is sometimes tough. We're past the stage of oogie-boogie readings. We don't burn candles for people in order for them to ward off enemies. We don't reveal when a person is going to die, have an accident, or lose a loved one. Palmistry is about life—and living it in the best and fullest sense possible.

—Rita Robinson
October 2001

CHAPTER 1

ANDS REVEAL GENETIC

INFLUENCES

The bond that links your true family is not one of blood,
but of respect and joy in each other's life.
Rarely do members of one family
grow up under the same roof.

—Richard David Bach, author

Genetic research is not just about the physical self. Scientists at a German university may have said it best when they described the connection between the hands and consciousness as the hands being "a direct tool of our consciousness." Given today's genetic research, a great deal of that consciousness, as applied to personality traits, may be inherited just as hair and eye color and body shapes are. With this in mind, it's not unrealistic for children's hands to show similarities to their parents' or extended family members' hands. We often hear someone say, "He's just like his father." The reference usually isn't about just body shape. Rather, it refers to the way the child behaves or reacts to events. Research even shows that whether a person likes or dislikes roller coasters may be an inherited trait, linked to the idea that some people may be predisposed to need the type of brain stimulation the ride provides.

Shyness, aggression, altruism, and helpfulness are some of these inherited characteristics, so it's not unrealistic for children's hands to show similarities to their parents or extended family members.

Driving across country one time on vacation, I saw what was obviously a mother and daughter, in their 50s and 20s respectively, sitting together on a bench at the Chicago Library. I was struck by how much they looked alike, even the way they held their heads at an angle. They both had the same look of contentment, even joy, on their faces, and both wore similar floppy brimmed hats decorated with brightly colored flowers. Their hand gestures were similar when they talked.

I had been so taken by them that I walked up to where they were sitting and asked if they were mother and daughter, and if many people asked them that. They laughed and said, "Yes. All the time." Then I asked if I could take their picture. (Being a tourist, I had a camera slung over my shoulder.)

They agreed, nearly in unison. Today, instead of taking a picture of their faces and bodies sitting on that bench, I would have asked to take photos of their hands, because they were sure to be similar, showing certain character and personality traits.

When we study the hands of different family members, we might be surprised at some of the likenesses in size, shape of thumbs and fingers, and many of the lines on the palm.

Knowing ourselves

Most of us have far more talents than we think we do, and a majority of our relatives, friends, and acquaintances are far more diversified than we might suspect, even when we've known them for years.

We never really know another person, and when we think we know, we're only using our own lens and capturing the essence of what we frame. Someone else, even the person in question, may have entirely different views. Palm readers provide another perspective, usually one far more objective than the one held by the individual or that person's friends, relatives, or business associates.

Palm readers have a far easier time reading the hands of people they've never met. For those we're familiar with, we often read the hands with preconceived biases.

Personalities and temperaments

The interest today in researching one's ancestry may be, in part, an outgrowth of the realization that we are our ancestors. Native populations have always acknowledged and honored their ancestry. During prayer, ceremony, or unplanned moments of sacredness or enlightenment they will say, "All of my relations...A-Ho." Many oriental cultures also honor their ancestors. At the family altar, the Butsudan may communicate with the dead.

Given that genetic research has shown how genes passed down through the ages shape us today, it should come as no surprise that some of these likenesses related to our relatives, living and dead, will show up in our hands.

Where do the lines come from?

The major creases in the hand, called the head, heart, life, and fate lines by palmists (and called flexion creases by medical scientists), are formed in the womb and discernible by the 12th week of fetal development. Prenatal testosterone that flows over the developing fetus in the first trimester of pregnancy influences the developing brain's neurological circuitry. During this same period, testosterone also stimulates the production of nerve growth factor, which affects the body's nervous system, and epidermal growth factor, which affects the skin of the body, including the hands.

Sonograms of the developing fetus at this 12- to 14-week period show not only the major lines, but also skin ridge patterns, including fingerprints. Thus, many of our characteristics and temperaments are shaped before we breathe our first breath. What we do with those characteristics and traits is another matter.

Just as a single marking on the hand doesn't tell a complete story, a single gene doesn't produce a certain behavior or endow a person with a particular trait. In other words, there is not a lone gene responsible for shyness and another gene for aggression. It is the interaction of our inherited traits, plus the environment and the culture, that determines how we react to and perceive life.

Edward O. Wilson, distinguished professor emeritus of biology at Harvard University, and author of the 1970's book, *Sociobiology,* argues that humans behave largely according to rules written in their very genes, although to what degree is still being debated among scientists.

Survival traits

Personality traits and their complements that have high genetic components across cultures include extroversion or introversion; agreeableness or irritability; conscientiousness or carelessness; emotional stability or anxiousness and excitability; and openness or closedness to new experiences. These traits are universal, because they may be related to survival. Other genetic traits that appear to be heritable are also emerging, including some from twin studies at the universities of Minnesota and Louisville showing that religiosity is influenced by genes.

Researchers at Oxford University discovered DNA links for father-to-son inheritance of priestly status among the tribe of Levi in Jewish tradition, heralding back to Aaron, brother of Moses.

Basically, though, genetics not only manifests itself in temperaments, but it can predispose a person to baldness, tall or short stature, and certain health problems. We can even inherit a predisposition to being a morning or an evening person.

It's now evident from genetic studies that predispositions exist for certain types of cancer, high blood pressure, diabetes, and several congenital abnormalities, many of which display themselves on the hand. We often become more aware of these inherited traits, such as being prone to an illness or a receding hair line, as we age, and it's not unusual to hear people say, "The older I get the more I become like my mother/father."

Sometimes, the chosen affiliation is wishful thinking. A woman may have liked her father more than the mother and will claim to be more like the father when, in reality, she resembles the mother more, not only in looks, but also in temperament, which may be evident in the markings and formations of the hand. (See Chapter 6 for more information.)

Marriage, friends, and genes

The inborn traits that ensure survival of the species are, according to some scientists, the ones that continue to be passed down through generations. Such inheritance is often accomplished by sons and daughters who marry people with traits similar to their own. Studies show that usually people from a young age select environments that they find stimulating and compatible in the areas of sports, scholarship, and relationships. Exceptions always exist, but most sons and daughters look for characteristics shared by their parents in selecting mates, especially if those traits have proven successful in their own families.

These same characteristics can be influenced by the family, but studies indicate that environmental influences do not make children in the same family similar. They all have their own distinct personalities, and parents can do little to change it, although they can nurture what is already present so that the children can function well in society.

Culture, too, plays a major role in shaping children and, later, influencing them as adults. Stanford University evolutionist Paul R. Ehrlich pointed out at the 2001 meeting of the American Institute of Biological Sciences in Arlington, Virginia, that the brain "is the only organ in the body that requires enormous input of information from the environment, including especially the cultural environment, in order to develop properly. And the amount of non-genetic information (culture) to which people are exposed is vastly greater than the store of genetic information in the human genome."

So we are both nature and nurture.

What can we change?

We may possess the ability to change dramatically, but only in the context of who we are to begin with. If we are born shy, and the best indicator of that is a very short little finger, not reaching the first phalange (or joint) on the ring finger (the finger of Apollo), we may overcome it through practice and persistence, but the trait will always be with us.

Shyness affects about 15 percent of the population and is considered one of the strongest of hereditary characteristics, although not all shy people are equally shy, and they exhibit their shyness in a variety of ways.

Thus, people can be shy, yet very assertive in some situations. Or shy people may exhibit shyness only around certain groups of people. Nor must shyness be the handicap Western societies perceive it to be, because being overly assertive or aggressive can often result in negative consequences. In some Asian countries, as well as some Native American cultures, shyness is considered a positive trait. Even so, individuals in all cultures who are considered shy can be very assertive if need be.

Many psychologists believe that shy children are often more sensitive to other people. They pay attention to others and often possess great observational skills.

What many palm readers try to achieve is to show that most characteristics and traits, such as shyness, if nurtured and used to the advantage of the person, are powerful and productive.

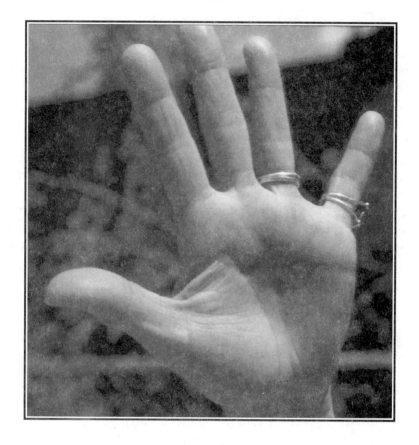

Graphic #1. Mother.

Graphics #1 and 2. *Mother and daughter. Fran Dancing Feather, a Native American Catholic and visionary, has a relatively short little finger for the size of her hands and in comparison to the rest of the fingers. She has performed as an entertainer and is in demand as a speaker and teacher. Her work as an artist and writer, though, provide her with hours of solitude, which she cherishes. She acknowledges that she sometimes has a difficult time being around people, and even at gatherings she will wander off by herself when the crowd gets too much for her. Sometimes she even "hides out," she says. Some of the other characteristics*

Graphic #2. Daughter.

of her hand—the strong arching thumb, the heavily jointed fingers, and the independent nature, as shown by the wide space between the ring finger and the little finger—provide other attributes that diminish the effects of the short little finger and possibly shyness.

Her daughter, Danielle, whose hand is also shown here, has some of her mother's characteristics, such as the short little finger in relation to the rest of the fingers and strong thumbs. At age 14, Danielle held a purple belt in karate. Her goal was to have a black belt by her senior year in high school.

Why certain characteristics predominate

We carry the same genes as our prehistoric ancestors, because they foster survival. Therefore, traits such as aggression and helpfulness, both of which promote survival in tribes, groups, cultures, and societies, are still evident. As a particular trait becomes useless or undesirable for survival in a given population, such as an overabundance of aggression, it can be weeded out.

In other words, just as palmistry isn't fatalistic, genes don't control all human behavior, even though we may be predisposed in one direction or the other. We may have certain personality traits, but the majority of the world's population is no longer made up of hunter–gatherers, who required certain skills that are no longer viable, so we're vastly capable of change. We can, if we so choose, take the character traits we may be born with, and use them in a positive way.

These traits often show in the shapes of the fingers or certain lines on the palm, but never by just one marking. It takes putting them together to determine if the person is, say, assertive. A couple of indications for that, which will be explored further in subsequent chapters, could be an exceptionally long index finger coupled with a long little finger, and a line of heart (the top horizontal line on the palm) that ends beneath the index finger, or that travels up into it.

How do we get the genes we have?

Each human cell has 23 pairs of chromosomes; half of each pair comes from the father and the other half from the mother. Genes are segments of chromosomes that contain the instructions for everything from eye color to baldness or from what is called an "easy child" to an aggressive one, although most characteristics are dependent on more than one gene or gene pair. A dominant gene will normally dominate a recessive gene.

A genotype is the actual genetic message, and the phenotype is the observable characteristics that result from the genotype.

Other factors, too, play a role in potential likenesses or differences in families. Theoretically, a child's genes should be a 50-50 mix of the genes carried by the parents, but mutations occur with approximately one child in 20. This means that part of the child's genetic makeup will differ from that of either parent, according to researchers at the University of Southern California.

This brief description of the genetic influence is a generalized approach, but genetic influence lays the foundation for much of our behavior, likes and dislikes, talents, health, and looks. It's important material for a palm reader, because we can see the influence of an individual's family of birth, if it is known. Frequently we read the hands of adoptees, and the scenario is changed, because we are dealing with characteristics of the family who raised them as well as some potential inherited characteristics. This can be done by comparing the dominant hand to the non-dominant hand. The non-dominant hand usually serves as a guide to hereditary tendencies that might show up in the dominant hand. (See Chapter 2 for more on dominant versus non-dominant hands.)

Keep in mind, however, that although dramatic likenesses have been found in studies of twins who were raised in separate families, vast differences also exist.

Family traits in sports

Individuals who excel in sports more than likely inherited the necessary winning genetic combinations, both mental and physical, from their parents. Additionally, the inherited tendencies can be nurtured by the ongoing influence of parents who are (or have been) involved in sports themselves, and who nurture and support their offspring in those same endeavors.

One only has to look at the top names in American football and baseball to see the connection. Ken Griffey Jr., son of Ken Griffey, formerly of the Seattle Mariners, plays for the Cincinnati Reds; the father of Barry Bonds of the San Francisco Giants, Bobby Bonds, played for the Pittsburgh Pirates; Tom Harmon led the way for his son Mark Harmon, now an actor, to play for the University of Southern California; Archie Manning, formerly of the New Orleans Saints, now watches his son, Peyton Manning, on the field for the Indianapolis Colts. There's no doubt that the influence of the sports figure parent also played a role in the child's interest in sports, but to become a national sports figure takes certain natural inborn characteristics, both physical and mental.

Utah Jazz head coach Jerry Sloan said after the Chicago Bulls beat the Jazz, "No one has hands like Michael Jordan." He described them as not only big, with long fingers that can manipulate the ball, but also "quick" and "soft," which adds even more to his prowess with the basketball.

Sloan also credited John Stockton and Karl Malone, both players for the Jazz, with having great hands for basketball. They both have large, arching thumbs and long fingers.

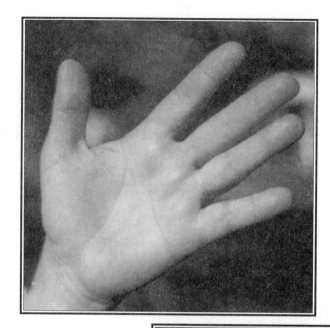

**Graphic #3.
Mother.**

**Graphic #4.
Father.**

Graphics #3, 4, 5, 6, 7, and 8. *The hands of the father, mother, and two sons shown here are examples of athletic hands. Also included on page 28 are the hands of an aunt (paternal side of family) and grandfather to show some of the same traits. Also note the likeness of the aunt and the grandfather, who are father and daughter.*

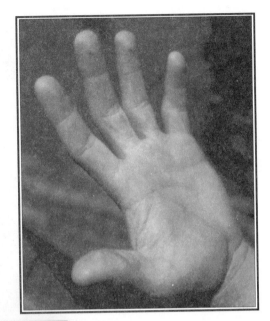

**Graphic #5.
Son A.**

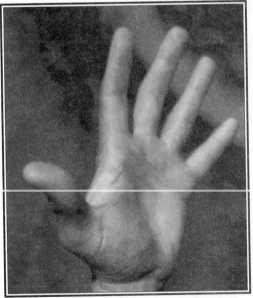

**Graphic #6.
Son B.**

Most notable are the large and long thumbs and the long, strong fingers of all family members. The grandfather, aunt, and two sons also possess the large arch between the index finger and thumb. Additionally, the thumb tips of the grandfather, aunt (his daughter), and two grandsons bend into a noticeable arch.

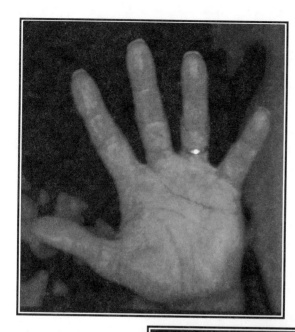

**Graphic #7.
Aunt.**

**Graphic #8.
Grandfather.**

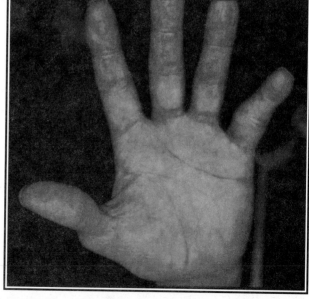

Both the mother and father of the two young athletes excelled in sports from an early age, and the sons followed in their footsteps. In other words, then, development of a child is both nature and nurture. These types of large fingered and thumbed hands are common in the country's top ball-playing athletes, especially basketball.

Nature and/or nurture

But what of an athlete who gets no backing from the family? Or a writer, dancer, or artist? Neuroscientists believe that further brain development remains greatly malleable throughout childhood and that, given stimulation and enrichment through lifetime learning, it can repeatedly blossom anew. And some people manage to overcome the obstacles of childhood on their own.

Many people of achievement have found other mentors throughout their lives, even if they were bereft of them in early childhood. Frequently, these will show up as lines of influence inside the line of life on the mount of Venus that surrounds the thumb. They are short horizontal lines that run from the thumb side of the hand toward the line of life, but they don't cross the line.

Some, though, with great potential have been so stunted by harsh non-nurturing environments that they fail despite outside help.

It isn't just achievement that is affected by nurturing, or non-nurturing environments. Studies show that a child raised in a harsh environment may overdose on stress hormones, causing the brain's circuitry to neglect activity that regulates joy and happiness. A child raised in a calm and loving atmosphere develops extraordinary circuitry in the parts of the brain that manifest an even, joyous temperament.

Although few humans escape stress, tragedy, disappointments, and other types of adversity, an even temperament to smooth the bumps seems to dispose some to bounce back more rapidly. When reading the hand, we look for this balance on the palm with such markings as clearly delineated lines, pink-toned skin, tactful pads on the fingertips, and a general open look to the hand.

Fingerprints

Although no two handprints are alike, in the same way that no two fingerprints are the same (not even in identical twins), certain fingerprint patterns can be found in the hands of family members, and some research indicates that certain types of patterns show up more frequently in various ethnic groups.

Fingerprints—more specifically the friction ridges that make up the prints—were studied in many ancient cultures, entertaining the idea that certain personality characteristics can be attributed to what are now referred to as various types of whorls, arches, and loops on the fingertips, and other parts of the palm. (See Graphic #9 following.)

The ancients were also intrigued by the likenesses of dermal patterns in family members. Scientific studies, though, didn't begin until a little more than one hundred years ago and moved forward after the publication in 1892 of *Finger Prints* by anthropologist Francis Galton, a cousin of Charles Darwin.

Today, many branches of science advance the understanding of ridge formations on the hands, including biology, neurology, and psychology. In addition to regular fingerprint patterns that we all carry, anomalies in prints also make news.

Three generations of one family with no discernible fingerprints have been described in fingerprint studies. Henry W. Baird III wrote in the 1964 edition of *Journal of Pediatrics* about a family in which the grandfather, his three children, and his nine grandchildren lacked the normal dermal ridges that make up fingerprints. The abnormality was believed due to an inherited epidermal condition (epidermolysis).

Long before scientific studies were conducted, however, ancient Chinese developed their own pattern interpretations, based on a single whorl pattern possible on each fingertip. They are as follows:

▸ Whorl pattern on one fingertip means you'll be poor.

▸ Whorl pattern on two fingertips means you'll be rich.

▸ Whorl pattern on three or four fingertips means open a pawnshop.

▸ Whorl pattern on five fingertips means be a go-between.

▸ Whorl pattern on six fingertips means be a thief.

▸ Whorl pattern on seven fingertips means you'll meet calamities.

▸ Whorl pattern on eight fingertips means eat chaff.

▸ Nine whorls and one loop, no work to do. Eat until you are old.

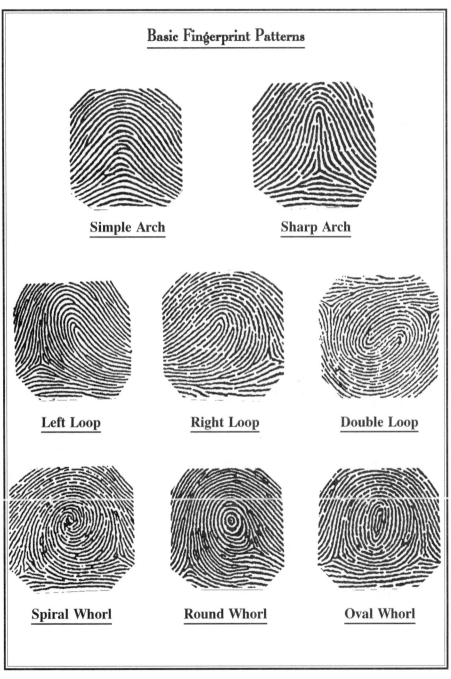

Graphic #9. Basic fingerprint patterns.

Basic fingerprint patterns

As well as being used for identification, the dermal ridge patterns on the fingertips are studied by a branch of medical science called dermatoglyphics as markers for predetermined, chronic illnesses and genetic abnormalities. Their studies also lead to the womb, because the patterns that are laid down by the 14th week of gestation last a lifetime and are altered on the surface only by the environment.

The alignment of the ridges is determined partly by genetics and partly by accidental or environmental stress and tension in the fetus during development. This occurs during that same critical period that testosterone is flowing over the fetus to affect the structures of the brain and the nervous system.

Although we are most familiar with the ridges that make up fingerprints, these same ridge patterns are found on the palm's volar pads (mounts). To the palmist, the pads are the mount of Venus (lying beneath the thumb); the mount of Luna on the percussion side of the hand (beneath the little finger on the lower part of the hand); those found beneath the fingers on the palm; and the area within the arch between the index finger and the thumb. They are also found at the side of the hand beneath the little finger. (See Chapter 7 for more information.)

Palmistry ridge and fingerprint patterns

Compare the fingerprints in the preceding Graphic #9 to determine what type is predominant on a person's hand.

- ▶ A simple arch is found on the hands of easy-going people.

- ▶ A sharp or tented arch belongs to those who have a difficult time expressing themselves, especially if the arch is found on the finger of Saturn.

- ▶ A tented arch stands for an emotional nature and is often found on the hand of an insecure person.

- ▶ Loops are found on the hands of sensitive people who are open to new ideas and ways of doing things.

- ▶ Double loops belong to especially energetic people (physically and mentally energetic).

- ▶ Whorls are found on the fingertips of very private, stoic individuals.

Everyone's palm is unique

In addition to fingerprints for identification, palm prints have also been used when no fingerprint patterns were discernible, as reported by Dick Clason in a 1985 edition of *The Print,* a professional fingerprint magazine. One of the first cases involved a stagecoach robbery in 1916. Among the evidence collected was a letter with a bloody palm print on it, allegedly belonging to the person on trial. The letter was presented in court and nearly thrown out as evidence. However, the judge allowed the prosecutor to take several palm prints from persons in court to show the differences, and the culprit was convicted of the crime.

This story shows that, although genetics plays a role in all human development (including the patterns on the hand and arrangement of dermal ridges), no two hands are alike.

We not only have telltale fingerprints and handprints, but those markings tell part of the story of who we are, what we're about, and what we're capable of.

Chapter 2

IGHT-HAND VS. LEFT-HAND DOMINANCE

Dominant and non-dominant hands

Determining whether a person is right- or left-handed is important in palm reading, because the dominant hand reflects what individuals make of the basic characteristics and attributes they were born with.

Part of this potential is shown in the non-dominant hand, because it becomes "the hand of birth." The non-dominant hand provides clues about the person's family, which parent the subject is most like, and either verifies or nullifies what is found in the dominant hand when compared.

Usually the dominant hand is the right hand; up to 90 percent of the population is right-handed. Left-handed individuals frequently possess special attributes, however, because handedness is linked to brain development.

Right-hand dominance

Several theories exist about why humans became predominantly right-handed. One theory is that when humans began to hunt and forage for food, it was necessary to develop specialized uses of one or the other hand. The brain followed suit, because it too is specialized. When humans began talking, it caused the predominant use of the right hand because speech is associated with the left hemisphere of the brain, which controls activity on the right side of the body. But that's only a theory. The distinction between the right and left sides of the brain being involved in specific tasks is falling out of favor with a growing number of scientists, who say that it's too simplistic to assign creative processes to the right side of the brain and technical skills and speech to the left side. They believe that the right and left sides work together, especially in language.

Some of the newer research also shows that language is intricately tied to use of the hands. The old saying about people not being able to talk without using their hands is more true than we ever imagined. Additionally, studies also show that words make up only 7 percent of communication; body language accounts for more than half of it.

When people aren't allowed to gesture, it interferes with communication and thought processes. Two blind people talking together use hand gestures.

What causes left-handedness?

It's believed that left-handedness can be manifested in the womb by trauma or caused by stress at birth. Studies have shown that during times of war or depressions, the incidence of left-handedness at birth increases.

On the genetic front, if both parents are right-handed, there is less than a 10-percent chance that they will produce a left-handed child. If one parent is left-handed, the chances of the child being left-handed climbs to near 20 percent, and if both parents are left-handed, the odds rise to about 26 percent.

Still, some theories attribute left-handedness to the way a mother carries the baby after birth, such as using the left hip for balance, or to customs in certain countries, such as not being allowed to eat with the left hand.

Even though many theories exist regarding whether or not (or how much) emphasis can be placed on inherited qualities of left-handedness, the following people, all from England, are left-handed:

▶   Queen Victoria.

▶   King George II.

▶   Queen Elizabeth, the Queen Mother.

▶   King George VI.

▶   Queen Elizabeth II.

▶   Prince Charles.

▶   Prince William.

Another interesting finding by psychologist Stanley Coren of the University of British Columbia shows that fingerprint patterns (see Graphic #9 in Chapter 1) between right- and left-handers are different. Left-handers have simpler patterns, with more arches and whorls. They also tend to have radial loops, which are rarer. Radial loops are found in the center of the fingerprint and are akin to a "u" that tilts toward the little finger. They are also found on a few right-handed individuals, but the chances of left-handedness are doubled when radial loops appear.

Other possible causes, though, still intrigue investigators. A University of Oxford study in 1999 showed an apparent tendency for left-handedness to be more prevalent in births that occur during March through July than from August through February. It's hypothesized that the relation between handedness and season of birth may be linked to seasonal variation of other factors, such as the incidence of infectious agents that strike populations at certain times of the year. One example is the flu, which is predominant in the fall and winter months when the fetus is developing for its subsequent birth in the March–July period.

Another theory holds that a specific dominant gene may be responsible for right-hand dominance, and when it's lacking, which it is in about 20 percent of the population, those people have a 50-50 chance of being either right- or left-handed. In other words, half of the 20 percent could be the approximate 10 percent of the population that turns up left-handed.

Going back even further, though, tools made prior to the Bronze Age show that people had no preference for their right or left hands, according to some archeological evidence. After that time, however, a preference for the right hand emerges. And it's estimated that about one-third of early American Indians were lefties, or at least ambidextrous.

So take your pick of theories. What is certain is that with all the genetic research taking place, we may eventually know what causes left-handedness. In the meantime, handedness plays a role in palm reading.

Left-handedness

When reading a left-handed person's palm, a few of the rules change, because we're usually dealing with a more creative person from the start. It also appears true, though, that lefties suffer greater incidences of reading disabilities, stuttering, autism, schizophrenia, dyslexia, immune diseases, migraines, allergies, eczema, and some categories of mental retardation.

However, they also generate higher proportions of architects, engineers, math teachers, writers, artists, astronauts, chess masters, inventers, sports figures, musicians, and other notables in proportion to the general population.

At least seven 20th-century presidents are/were lefties. They are:

▶ James Garfield.

▶ Herbert Hoover.

▶ Harry S Truman.

▶ Gerald Ford.

▶ Ronald Reagan.

▶ George H. Bush.

▶ Bill Clinton.

Some noted historical figures were also left-handed. These include:

▶ Joan of Arc.

▶ Alexander the Great.

▶ Charlemagne.

▶ Julius Caesar.

▶ Napoleon Bonaparte.

▶ Albert Einstein.

▶ Henry Ford.

▶ Helen Keller.

▶ Dr. Albert Schweitzer.

The numbers of noted left-handed sports figures, actors, musicians, artists, and writers number in the thousands and range from Nate Archibald (basketball) to Ted Williams and Tommy Lasorda to boot (baseball). Stars include June Allyson and Bruce Willis, as well as novelists James Baldwin and Eudora Welty. Artists run the gambit from Leonardo da Vinci to Paul Klee. Not to be slighted are comedians: George Burns, Carol Burnett, and Jay Leno. And in what category does southpaw Oprah Winfrey fit?

You will find that more men are on long lists of noted left-handers, because left-handedness affects twice as many men as women.

Left-handed folklore and bias

Some of the older meanings associated with left-handedness have left their scars. A left-handed compliment is deemed an insult; a left-handed marriage stands for an adulterous sexual liaison; a left-handed wife means a mistress; an illegitimate baby might be from the left side of the bed; a left-handed business means something illegal; and an unlucky person might be baptized by a left-handed priest.

These connotations might seem strange to us now, but lefties, up until the past few years, were subjected to insults. In some societies, left-handers were considered omens of bad luck.

Unfortunately, some of this bias crept into ancient palmistry classics and has been rewritten and passed on in newer texts.

Right- and left-hand readings

For people who are right-handed, take a look at both palms to determine any differences in them. If, for instance, the lines appear deeper and more distinct in the right hand, it is a clue that the person probably has achieved a full life and made use of at least some of his or her inherent talents. An opposite reading (left dominant and right non-dominant) would be called for if the person is left-handed.

If the lower portion of the left hand (on a right-handed person) near the wrist and the line of life generally contains a great many small lines descending from the line of life, it often signifies a troubled childhood. If the jumble of lines is not present on the right hand (in this case, the dominant hand), then the person has overcome the childhood obstacles.

Often the lines are very different between the right and left palms. For instance, the lines of life and head may be joined on the thumb side of the hand on either the left or right hand and separated on the other. If the person is right-handed, and the left hand shows the lines joined, it would indicate that the person's inborn nature is to be more conservative, but through some circumstances, he or she became more of a risk-taker as an adult. The reader would search the hand for other signs to see what caused this type of change.

Another manifestation that shows frequently when comparing the right and left hands is a wider arch between the thumb and index finger on one hand. The wider that arch, the more nonjudgmental and accepting the

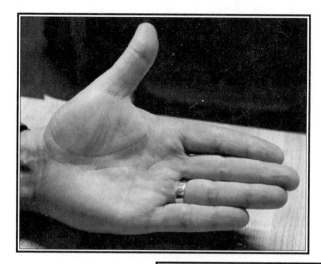

Graphic #10.
Left hand.

Graphic #11.
Right hand.

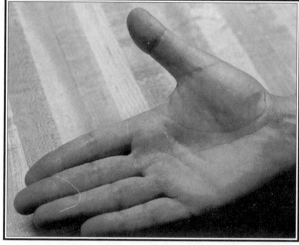

Graphics #10 and 11. *The right and left hands of the same man, showing differences in the lines of life and head. In these two prints, the left hand, which is this person's hand of birth (non-dominant), shows the lines of head and life joined at the beginning beneath the index finger (Jupiter) about midway between it and the thumb. The line of life runs down the hand, surrounding the mount beneath the thumb, and the line of head runs nearly horizontally across the palm. In the same position on the man's dominant right hand, the two lines are separated, indicating a radical change in his life. What it indicates on this man's hand is that as a child he was a great deal more shy and introverted, but eventually, he overcame some of the trauma of his childhood and began to develop a far more assertive attitude. He also overcame a great many inborn fears. (See Chapter 6 for more on the separated lines of life and head.)*

person is of others. An arch that is wider on the dominant hand and very tight on the non-dominant hand indicates that the person has probably outgrown the prejudices or judgmental attitudes of the parents.

As more is learned about reading the hand, many comparisons can be made between the dominant and non-dominant hands concerning where people are coming from and where they are headed. By initially studying both hands, the reader can tell whether individuals have made full use of their natural abilities and if they have surpassed the markings of the non-dominant, or "birth," hand, whether it be the right or left one.

What about people who use both hands?

Artists such as Michelangelo often painted with both hands; Benjamin Franklin signed the Declaration of Independence and the Constitution with his left hand, to name just two notables who grace the environs of lefties or of the ambidextrous. Actually, Franklin was born left-handed, but his teachers, as was common in those days, smacked his hands whenever he used his left hand.

Medical scientists speculate that lefties and ambies exercise their brains more and grow more cells. Their corpus callosums (the bundle of nerves that join the right and left hemispheres of the brain) are approximately 11 percent larger than those of right-handed people. An autopsy of Albert Einstein's (believed to have been a leftie) brain also showed larger profusions of superficial capillaries interlacing the cerebral cortex than the average brain, as well as additional glial cells. The central nervous system consists of nearly equal parts of neurons and glial cells, with the glial cells providing support and protection for the neurons.

The ability to use both hands can be a plus in many occupations, including sports, and it can spur creativity. If you're right-handed, try drawing a picture with your left hand. It might not be as perfectly drawn, but it will be more creative. Many books on boosting creativity suggest that people draw or write with the non-dominant hand.

How important is all this to palmistry?

Because handedness involves the brain, it adds clues to the overall reading, because the lines and formations and the way we hold and use our hands are all connected to the brain.

To test how the brain works in conjunction with the hand, hold either hand flat, and realign the fingers by twisting the flat palm so that the ring finger becomes longer than the index finger. In order to do that, you need to think about it first. If a technician were monitoring an MRI (magnetic resonance imaging) to scan your brain at the same time (that you twist your palm), a portion of the brain associated with each movement would light up. It's another example of how malleable our brains, and our hands, are and how the hands and brain interact with one another. If, say, a palm reading showed that a person tended to be judgmental of others and that person wanted to change, the thumb and the space between it and the index finger could be exercised to make it more flexible. The action, though, requires thought. We think, *I don't want to be judgmental, and I am going to do something about it.* So the action of increasing the flexibility of the hand makes the thinking more flexible.

By our physical action, we affect our mental action and thoughts.

Birth hand and the inner life

The non-dominant (or birth) hand can provide clues to individuals' inner lives, because although they may have overcome some of the characteristics they were born with, such as shyness, aggression, a fear of taking risks, and so forth, a particular trait may still dog them occasionally.

Many people who are adept at performing or speaking in front of groups may have been shy in childhood (as shown by a short little finger, among other things). Some might have experienced problems with stuttering, but, through training and resolve, they now appear to be "naturals" in front of audiences. Occasionally, though, they fall back into their childhood shyness and find it nearly impossible to perform.

The resolve people have used to overcome characteristics such as shyness has become one of their strengths and may show up in the hands, usually by comparing the non-dominant hand to the dominant one.

One of the most important functions of a palm reading is to make the predominant part of any reading geared to the strengths a person already has—or is capable of developing. This is true whether you're reading your own hand, or that of another.

When the dominant hand is more developed than the non-dominant hand, it shows that the person has taken advantage of inborn strengths and talents and made the most of any advantages he or she was provided early in life.

Quite the opposite is true if the dominant hand does not show that the individual has taken advantage of inherited and nurtured strengths that were available as shown in the non-dominant hand. The individual needs to be made aware of these traits in order to fulfill the possibilities shown in the hand.

A non-dominant hand that shows far weaker lines, mounts, and other markings than the dominant hand can be a sign that the person really made an attempt to overcome a none-too-enriching childhood. However, some differing marks between the two hands can indicate that the person has simply changed what is valued. Perhaps his or her parents were financially poor, and the person has become wealthy, or the parents were less educated, and the son or daughter received a fine education. In these instances, parents may have provided the means for their children to enjoy better material lives than they did. So the reading in no way is meant to be a put-down on the part of the parents.

Comparing the two hands at the onset of the reading simply supplies the reader with background knowledge of the person. It is a touchstone, a starting point.

Markings to note for comparisons

As you study the differences in your two hands, make note of the following, which are explained in subsequent chapters on lines, markings, formations, and finger shapes. It's extremely rare that the shape of the palm or the fingers will be different in an individual's right and left hands, but the lines and numerous markings can be very different. Here's what you should note:

▶ The lines of life, head, and heart (their depth, color, endings, and beginnings).

▶ Changes in the line of fate from one hand to the other.

▶ Differences in the spaces between fingers.

▶ Differences in the space between the thumb and index finger.

▶ Differences in the great triangle and the quadrangle.

▶ Minor lines that appear on the dominant hand but not the non-dominant one.

▶ Changes in the flexibility of one hand over the other.

 HAND SHAPES AND TEXTURES

Other parts of the body assist the speaker but the
hands speak themselves. By them we ask, promise, invoke, dismiss,
threaten, entreat, deprecate. By them we express fear, joy, grief,
our doubts, assent, or penitence; we show moderation or profusion
and mark number and time

—Quintilian, first century Roman rhetorician

Hand structure

The hands have the greatest agility of any part of the body. The palmaris logus, a long slender muscle of the forearm, flexes the hand, and the palmar aponeurosis serves as the connective tissue surrounding the muscles of the palm. The metacarpal artery feeds blood to the fingers, and branches of the brachial, which is the main artery of the upper arm, provide blood to the hands. More than a dozen other veins and arteries also supply blood to the hands, making them powerful tools of work and love, plus strong indicators of a person's energy levels.

When energy is dissipated, the fingers of the hand draw inward, and the sponginess of the hand becomes flaccid. The Earth mount, which lies on the outside of the palm near the arch between the thumb and index finger, also flattens and becomes less solid when we're feeling down. It's easy to check by pressing the straight thumb against the side of the straight

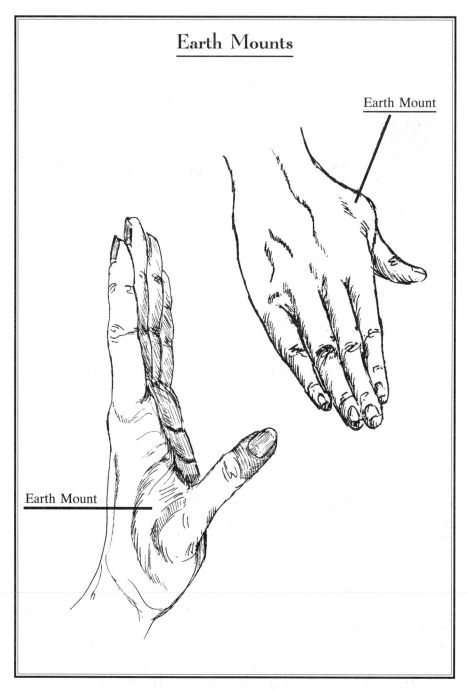

Graphic #12. Earth mounts.

index finger and then testing the solidity of the mount as it takes shape. The mount arises on the back of the hand near the thumb as it pushes against the side of the index finger. (Do not bend the fingers.) It changes with our energy levels: It's solid when we're full of energy and soft when our energy level is weak.

Changing shapes

Just as times change and so do a society's sensibilities, palmistry has followed much the same route. It has changed through the ages, particularly as it was dispersed into a variety of cultures, only to have their own spin placed on what constituted a "good" hand.

Palmistry, from its ancient beginnings—wherever that may be (some experts say India, others claim Persia or China, and others say Egypt)—has touched most societies. Cultures where long-fingered individuals seemed to be in the upper class, naturally influenced the perception that perhaps long-fingered individuals were smarter, more gifted, and luckier. Societies where shorter-fingered individuals appeared to have the greatest survival skills may have considered short, full hands the most desirable.

The foundations of ancient palmistry must, of course, be considered, but palmistry for today's students needs more flexibility and updating to maintain relevance in today's ever-changing world. Palm readers no longer just speak of women meeting a tall, dark stranger. Women might be just as interested in their careers. Men aren't restricted to one type of profession. The majority of the industrialized world maintains freedom of movement, so people travel and experience more. Over the years, palmistry has built on itself, adding new truths and discarding those that no longer speak to a knowledgeable populace. The end result is that palmistry isn't just about predictions; it's about human potential and understanding. Dermatoglyphics is a branch of medical science that studies the skin ridges and patterns for inherited diseases; a few psychologists use pressure points on the hands of patients to probe the subconscious; and professions of all sorts study hand movements for clues to a person's temperament, personality, and capabilities. Politicians and other public speakers are trained to use specific hand movements for peak audience response.

For purposes of hand reading, though (and a reading involves the entire hand), the palm shapes provide the foundation, measured from the base of the fingers to just above the top of the wrist, and from the percussion side of the hand beneath the little finger, to the bottom of the thumb.

The four hand shapes

Ancient palmistry referred to about seven types of hand shapes, and sometimes more, but many of today's palmists use four main categories, linked to the four Elements, or four main metaphysical designations: Earth, Air, Fire, and Water, which are often also referred to in the same order as square, philosophic, spatulate, and conic. (I will use a combined reference throughout this book.)

The four basic hand shapes refer only to the palm. The fingertip shapes are another matter and can put a very different spin on the hand reading. (See Chapter 5 for information about fingertips.)

Often, it's better to possess a mixed hand, which means that the shape of the palm might be Earth/square, but the fingertips could be conic (pointed).

For general purposes, the size of the palm has little bearing on a reading, as it usually reflects the person's body shape and type of hand. Air/philosophic hands tend to be larger than Earth/square. Fire/spatulate hands are about equal with Earth/square, and Water/conic is usually the smaller. The softness, malleability, strength, and energy of the hand are also important.

Consider the hands of two brothers, both chiropractors. One, tall and lanky, has very large, flexible hands. The other, short and stocky, has far smaller hands that are more rigid. They acknowledged that their father's hands had been large and flexible. It's more than likely that the stockier brother has hands similar to his mother's. Yet, both are chiropractors who go about their practices in entirely different manners.

Another man, a former newspaper reporter who quit his job and returned to college to obtain a Ph.D. in literature, was from a steel town in Pennsylvania. He was broad shouldered, long-armed, and stocky. His hands, long and elegant looking, did not match his body. It irritated him when I pointed out the disparity, but he later laughed about it, saying that one of his college professors, a small, feisty 80-year-old woman, had said the same thing.

The Earth/square palm

The Earth/square speaks to a palm that is nearly as broad as it is long. It is sturdy looking and belongs to people who are capable of hard work, whether physical or intellectual. The Earth/square hand appears neat and orderly, and even if other markings, such as pointed (conic) fingertips or full mounts (the raised portions beneath the fingers and surrounding the thumb and the side of the hand beneath the thumb; also see Chapter 7 for more information), bring out different traits, the basic personality will retain a solidness. People with Earth/square palms make loyal, trusting friends. As employees, they are hardworking and trustworthy.

A pure Earth/square hand, which is rare, includes square fingertips and fingers that are about the same length as the palm, with the thumb usually lacking a large, flexible arch between it and the index finger. When the arch lacks flexibility, the mounts are frequently underdeveloped, because the individual may be reluctant to step outside the boundaries he or she has established and to experience something different. Earth/square and Fire/spatulate hands usually don't compare to Water/conic or Air/philosophic hands with regard to mount size unless the entire Air/philosophic hand is thin when viewing it from the side.

People with such hands more often than not embody the extreme of the traits associated with Earth/square hands and become die-hard conformists, extreme conservatives, and religious fanatics. They may be labeled the "salt of the earth," but they miss out on a great deal because they are tied to custom, dogma, and safety.

But, as noted, pure Earth/square hands are rare. More likely, Earth/square hands are a combination involving Earth/square palms and a few conic fingertips.

Strong Earth/square hands embody some, but not all, of the following characteristics:

▶ Reliable.

▶ Hard-working.

▶ Believes in self.

▶ Willing to sacrifice.

▶ Loves the outdoors.

▶ Loyal.

▶ Stubborn.

▶ Persevering.

▶ Trustworthy.

▶ Energy-filled.

The downside of a pure Earth/square hand (palm and all fingers), carried to the extreme can include some, but not all, of the following characteristics:

▶ Dogmatic.

▶ Egocentric.

▶ Expects too much of others.

▶ Fanatic environmentalist or religious zealot.

▶ Never lets go.

▶ Restless.

▶ Judgmental.

Examples of notables with Earth/square palms

Cesar Chavez, labor leader and activist

Shirley MacLaine, actor, author

Rosie O'Donnell, actor, talk-show host, author

Bjorn Borg, tennis great

Michael Flatley, dancer, choreographer

Brad Pitt, actor

Woody Allen, actor, producer, writer

Vicente Fox, president of Mexico

Gray Davis, governor of California

George W. Bush, president of the United States

Kobe Bryant, basketball star

Tommy Lee Jones, actor

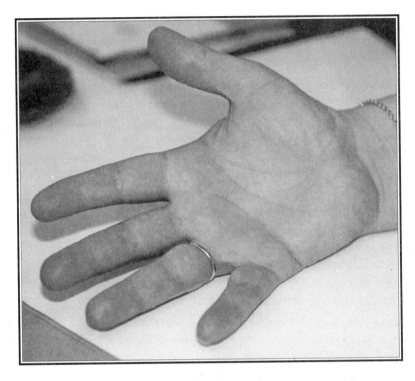

Graphic #13. Earth/square palm

Graphic #13. *This is an Earth/square palm with conic fingertips on the index and little fingers. Also, the mounts are full, so this is not a pure Earth/ square hand, as few are. The fingertips and mounts, to be discussed in following chapters, show this person to be highly energetic; artistic, as shown by the conic fingertips; and involved in a number of interests (the developed mounts). It needs to be noted that not all Earth/square hands are as full as this person's, nor the fingers as short. This is the hand of a highly creative individual who is the author of several children's books and the host of a radio show.*

The Air/philosophic palm

The Air/philosophic palm is at its finest when it's somewhat full with developed mounts and long fingers. The palm is far longer from the bottom of the fingers to just above the wrist than it is wide. It has many manifestations.

When it is fairly thick and strong-looking (viewed from the side), it belongs to highly intelligent, curious individuals. Air/philosophic hands often belong to people who live contemplative lives. They can be liberal or conservative but have a wide grasp and view of the world. They are definitely not small-minded.

If the palm of the philosophic hand is thin (again, viewed from the side) and the fingers long and thin, it can belong to individuals who are too trusting, idealistic, and sensitive. They don't have the energy of those with full, heavier-looking Air/philosophic hands. They can be just as intelligent as their counterparts with fuller hands, but they aren't as aggressive, assertive, or driven to reach goals. They aren't as sure of themselves as those with stronger Air/philosophic hands.

The strong Air/philosophic hand can be sensitive and idealistic, but it is also grounded in reality. People with these hands make good students, teachers, and philosophers. A good many world political and religious leaders possess Air/philosophic hands.

An Air/philosophic hand that is extremely thick and soft-looking, however, might not be the best formation to have. It is one that carries everything to extreme, even though highly intelligent and even crafty. It's as if the thoughts have been carried too far and become too heavy.

Strong Air/philosophic hands embody some, but not all, of the following characteristics:

▶ Curious.

▶ Inquisitive.

▶ Having intellectual pursuits.

▶ On a spiritual quest.

▶ Independent-thinking.

▶ Contemplative.

▶ Energy-filled.

▶ Sensitive.

▶ Idealistic.

Weak, thin-looking, or overly thick Air/philosophic hands might show some, but not all of the following characteristics:

▸ Gossipy.

▸ Zealous.

▸ Manipulative.

▸ Filled with hot and cold energy.

▸ Domineering.

▸ Having unused intelligence.

▸ Moody.

▸ Indecisive.

Examples of notables with Air/philosophic hands

Ronald Reagan, former president

Demi Moore, actor

Audrey Meadows, actor

Tommy Lasorda, baseball coach

Oprah Winfrey, talk-show host, entrepreneur

Diana, the late Princess of Wales

Bob Dole, politician

George McGovern, former presidential contender

Hillary Clinton, New York state senator, former first lady

George H. Bush, former president

Sandra Bullock, actor

Celine Dion, musician

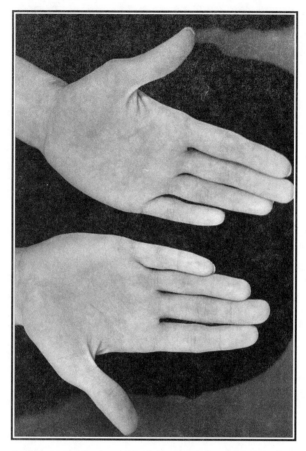

Graphic #14. Air/philosophic palms.

Graphic #14. *Strong Air/philosophic palms with square fingertips. This is the hand of an entertainer, a female magician, which is more rare than normal in the field of magic, which is dominated by men. Also take note of the strong thumb on her hand. (Thumbs will be discussed in Chapter 4.)*

A few of the not-so-desirable traits of the Fire/spatulate hand include some, but not all, of the following:

▶ Restlessness.

▶ Stubbornness.

▶ Moody.

▶ Has unfinished projects.

▶ Know-it-all.

▶ Carelessness.

▶ Forgetfulness.

Examples of notables with Fire/spatulate palms

Hussein bin Talal, former king of Jordan

Barbara Jordan, former congresswoman

Steven Spielberg, director, producer, screenwriter

Sharon Stone, actor

The Water/conic palm

Often called the "artistic hand," the Water/conic palm is medium-sized, with medium-length, tapered fingers and slightly pointed fingertips. It is a soft-looking hand, always full, and usually with smooth jointed fingers.

People with Water/conic hands tend to have a great appreciation of art in all its forms. They enjoy color and beauty and will try to surround themselves with art under any circumstances.

The Water/conic hand in its pure form retains this love of beauty but rarely produces it. For that to happen, the hand needs to incorporate other types of fingertips to provide the energy, strength, and discipline needed for personal achievement in the arts. The pure Water/conic hand is the "appreciator" of art in all its forms. The Water/conic palm with mixed fingers is the "doer" of art.

Water/conic people can be easily intimidated by others and are often swayed in their reasoning by friends and family. They can also be emotional, although they might hold those feelings inside until they bubble over, sometimes at inappropriate times. However, with other strong markings, such as square fingertips, strong lines, and well-developed mounts, they can be fierce, outspoken, determined, and disciplined.

The positive characteristics of the Water/conic hand, which usually involves a blend of other hand characteristics, include some, but not all, of the following:

▶ Naturally artistic.

▶ Generous.

▶ Loves beauty.

▶ Tender.

▶ Thoughtful.

▶ Creative.

▶ Sensitive.

▶ Gentle.

The peculiarities for owners of Water/conic hands to note include some, but not all, of the following:

▶ Overly emotional.

▶ Lazy.

▶ Has big ideas.

▶ Loves luxury.

▶ Is easily swayed.

▶ Holds in anger.

Examples of notables with Water/conic palms

Elizabeth Taylor, actress

Queen Latifah, entertainer

Al Gore, former vice-president

Ted Kennedy, senator

James Woods, actor

Cameryn Meinhem, actress

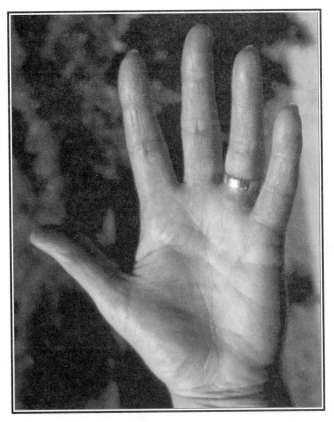

Graphic #17. Water/conic palm.

Graphic #17. *This Water/conic hand, with the middle and ring fingers slightly squared, belongs to a woman restaurateur who is also noted for her artwork. She also is adept at the piano, sings solos in an area chorus, and is very much involved in promoting art in the community in which she lives. She combines the love of the arts with the discipline for hard work that it takes.*

Other conditions to consider with palm shape

The shape of the palm lays the foundation for reading the palm, but other conditions, such as its color and the way it feels to the touch, are important.

In other chapters, the mounts (or fleshy pads on the palms), fingertips, thumb shapes, certain lines, and other markings will be discussed. Taken all together, the various markings and shapes portray a full picture of what a person's hands have to say about him or her.

Color of the palms

The palm's color reflects the mood, and even the health, of an individual. Also, room or outdoor temperature affects the color and feel of the hands.

Pink-tinged and mildly red palms that are warm and fairly elastic to the touch are usually the healthiest of all, showing good blood flow and calm temperament at the time of the reading.

Color, of course, can change dramatically. Anger brings on deep reds and even purples. Smokers usually have very red palms.

White, or pale palms, sometimes with a tinge of blue, are more often found on the hands of introverted personalities. If the hand is still fairly elastic to the touch, the person might be quite shy. A hard and cold palm portends an unsympathetic soul or a lack of energy.

Yellow-tinged palms are often found on worrywarts, pessimists, or anxiety-prone individuals, but other markings might point to the yellow tint being a temporary state. It can also be related to certain illnesses, such as jaundice.

Feel of the palm

Cold hands can indicate tension, self-doubt, fear, grief, and general unhappiness. Warm hands show good self-esteem and an upbeat mood. These hot or cold conditions are often tied to our autonomic nervous system, which frequently shows our state of mind, even when we try not to show emotion. It is the same system that causes us to blush when we don't want to and brings out goose bumps to the skin.

Ancient Earth signs regarding the feel of the hands mean the following:

▸ Earth/square: Hot and wet shows moodiness.

▸ Air/philosophic: Cold and dry shows cheerfulness.

▸ Fire/spatulate: Hot and dry shows a volatile personality.

▸ Water/conic: Cold and wet show a lack of emotion.

Hard and soft palms

The feel of a palm can offer clues to a person's temperament and personality, but the shape of the palm also has some bearing on how it feels. Those with Water/conic palms usually have softer, spongier hands, because they are fuller than, say, someone whose hands are Earth/square or Fire/spatulate, two types that tend to be firm. However, those same hands can be very spongy and full, which might offer other clues about them.

Most palmists look for a fairly firm, spongy, warm hand. Soft is okay, but when the hand feels plump and exceptionally soft, it often belongs to a self-indulgent person.

A hard, bony hand, if it's also warm to the touch, usually belongs to a person who is hard-working and generous. Palms that feel smooth, full, and warm belong to even-tempered people.

The skin on women's hands tends to be finer than the skin on men's hands, but not because of particular types of work. Most men are born with deeper skin ridges and wider spaces between the ridges on the palms, which makes them more deeply grooved. Both men and women have those patterns covering the palms, but some are simply smoother than others at birth. Also, finer skin ridges are usually found on Water/conic and Air/philosophic hands than on Earth/square or Fire/spatulate hands. As is the case with fingerprints, the skin-ridge patterns on the right and left palms of an individual are never exactly alike.

The ridges contain sweat glands and pores, which is why some people's hands sweat during temperature variations or when they become nervous.

If you've ever shaken a hand and thought it felt like a "wet fish" your observation is pretty accurate, although it has more to do with a droopy, listless feeling than just being wet. Some people can give a very hearty handshake that's still damp, indicating either nervousness or a hot day.

Those who shake hands with a firm grip display good self-esteem. However, if the handshake is overly firm and quick, it can mean that the person wants to get on to other things. If it's held too long, and the hand feels fleshy, the person might be trying to impress you, while at the same time feeling insecure.

Women entering the workforce are being encouraged to pay attention to their handshakes, which traditionally have been a little more listless than a man's firm grip, according to research by psychologists. Studies show that a firm handshake shows strength and vigor, especially when it lasts long enough and is combined with good eye contact. It was also found that an individual's handshake is consistent over time and is related to his or her personality.

People with firm handshakes are viewed as being more open to experience and less shy, so it may be beneficial to practice a good handshake before applying for a job.

CHAPTER 4

THUMBS

An entire chapter on the thumbs might at first appear extravagant, but the thumb is one of the strongest gauges of a person's temperament, personality, and strength. Thumbs are the first things that many professional palm readers notice. Poets, too, have taken notice of the thumbs, such as Carl Sandberg's *Musings of a Police Reporter in the Identification Bureau.*

> You have loved forty women, but you have only one thumb.
> You have led a hundred secret lives, but you mark only one thumb.
> You go round the world and fight in a thousand wars and
> win all the world's honors, but when you come back
> home the print of the one thumb your mother gave
> you is the same print of thumb you had in the old
> home when your mother kissed you and said good-by.
> Out of the whirling womb of time come millions of men
> and their feet crowd the earth and cut one another's
> throats for room to stand and among them all
> are not two thumbs alike.
> Somewhere is a Great God of Thumbs who can tell the
> inside story of this.

From *The Chicago Poems* (Henry Holt and Co., 1916)

Human development

One of the hallmarks that sets humans apart from most other animals, but that links us with some other primates, is the opposable thumb. It rotates on its axis and makes thumb pad–to–index finger touch possible. This enables humans to have fine-tuned grasping abilities. Another unique characteristic of the grasping thumb is that humans are able to concentrate for long periods of time using this motion, which makes it possible for us to create. In this creation, parts of the brain and hand work in tandem.

Additionally, stereoscopic vision and a grasping hand led to the eye-hand coordination of primates and, according to some theories, made it possible to survive the early habitats more efficiently than some other animals. Today, humans manipulate tools and their environments with more dexterity than other animals.

The abundance of muscles at or near the base of the thumb are responsible for its wide range of motion and also for the large mount beneath the thumb (Venus). The area contains more muscles than those beneath the fingers.

The chicken and the egg speculations plague the thumb. Which came first: the opposable thumb or a brain that wanted us to build fires, shelter, and tools?

However we look at it, though, the thumb was a healthy contributor to what we term as evolution.

For a simple, hands-on demonstration, tape the thumb to the index finger and try to attach a paper clip to several sheets of paper. Try to thread a needle. Try to write your name. Try to shave or put on mascara.

The thumb does a lot and says a lot.

From beginning to end

From cradle to grave, the thumb sets the tone for the life to be and the life lived. Life begins and ends with the grasp.

The grasp of a newborn's hand, which involves the thumb, often tells neonatal nurses how well the infant is doing. Many babies born premature or with medical conditions have very weak grasps. The thumb is held by the infant beneath the other fingers, as if for security. The weakness or disturbance may disappear as the infant gains strength, and the thumb will begin showing more action.

One popular observation is that children learn to use their forefingers and thumb together when their egos begin developing. A good-sized thumb and index finger are associated with strong egos, and short, weak thumbs indicate weaker egos.

When the tip of the thumb bends inward toward the palm, it can mean people who believe they are surrounded by so many obstacles that it's impossible to overcome them. This can be a temporary state.

In a continuum, the fingers of people on their deathbeds close in, grasping the thumb beneath them.

Thumb shapes

Large and medium, sturdy-appearing thumbs indicate energy, strong egos, and leadership ability.

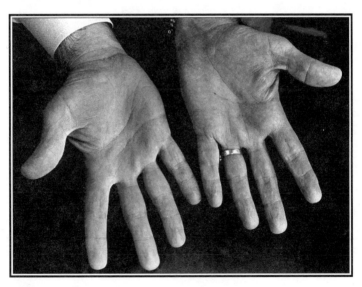

Graphic #18.

These are the hands of Ron Lurie, a former mayor of Las Vegas. The picture was taken when I was interviewed for an article in the Las Vegas Review Journal. *His was one of the palms I was sent to read without knowing whose hand it was. I reported, in part, that it was the hand of a multitalented individual with an outstanding sense of humor. Although his judgments may have seemed hasty to some, because he was quick on his feet, he would have given careful consideration to all his decisions.*

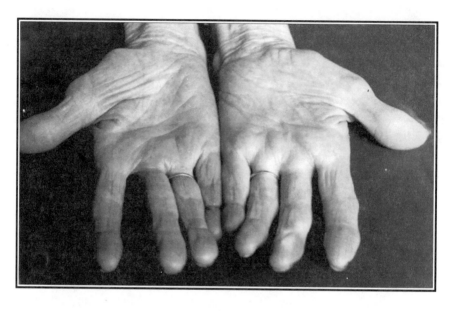

Graphic #19.

This graphic shows the hands of Leila, a woman who lived on her own until she reached the age of 105, at which time she was placed in a nursing home. Take notice of the strong, powerful thumbs in this photo that was taken when she was 102. She is a source of delight to many and has taught us a few things about what it takes to reach old age. For example, when she was in her hundreds, she was asked to speak at a local high school on the bombing of Pearl Harbor at the start of World War II. She had been there, so gladly accepted. After she accepted, she immediately made an appointment to get her hair and nails done. In the nursing home when I visited her, she spoke about how important it is for all of us to love one another. That love is the most wonderful thing about living.

Parts of the thumb

The thumb contains only two phalanges; the fingers contain three, divided by the joints. However, the thenar eminence, or mount of Venus, lying beneath the thumb on the palm can almost be considered part of the thumb, because the mount contains the strong muscles that control the thumb.

The first phalange

The first phalange on the tip of the thumb represents willpower. When the first phalange is longer than the one beneath it, which represents logic, the individual can be stubborn. Depending on other hand markings, it can also stand for determination and persistence.

If this tip, or first phalange, of the thumb is flat, however, it means that the person doesn't finish projects started. If the tip is bulbous (or club-shaped), it's a sign of a quick, hot, temper—a blind rage. People capable of this type of rage may, for the most part, be calm-tempered and even placid, but a rare hair-trigger temper can set them off.

The shapes of thumb tips take on double the meaning of fingertip shapes. Earth/square fingertips, as with the square hand, indicate a hard worker who wants to get things done immediately. If all the fingertips plus the thumb are square-tipped, the person is a taskmaster, not only for himself or herself, but also for others.

Fire/spatulate thumbs indicate ideas and imagination. But look for other fingertip shapes, because an all-spatulate hand can lead a person astray with too many ideas and not enough discipline to get the job done.

A Water/conic thumb shows the artistic side of people, whether they produce art themselves or possess an innate love of beauty and the aesthetics of life. Other markings will determine whether they are doers or observers.

No special designation exists for Air/philosophic fingertips because it refers to an elongated palm shape. Air/philosophic hands can incorporate square, spatulate-, or conic-shaped fingertips.

The second phalange

The second phalange, between the one standing for will and the mount of Venus, gives the person the ability for reaching conclusions based on logic. Usually by the time people with a second phalange give an opinion, they have weighed all sides and have a good grasp of what they are talking about. It doesn't necessarily mean they are correct in every instance, but they don't tend to shoot from the hip, and are therefore more rational in their conclusions.

Often, people with a long second phalange make good leaders, depending on other lines on the palm.

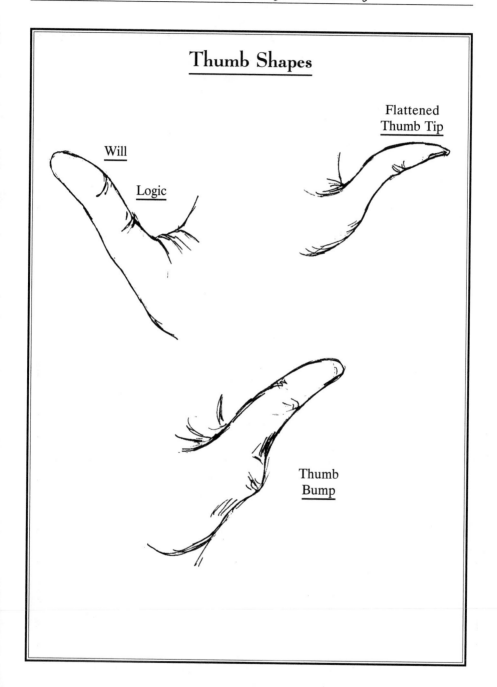

Graphic #20. *A variety of thumb shapes.*

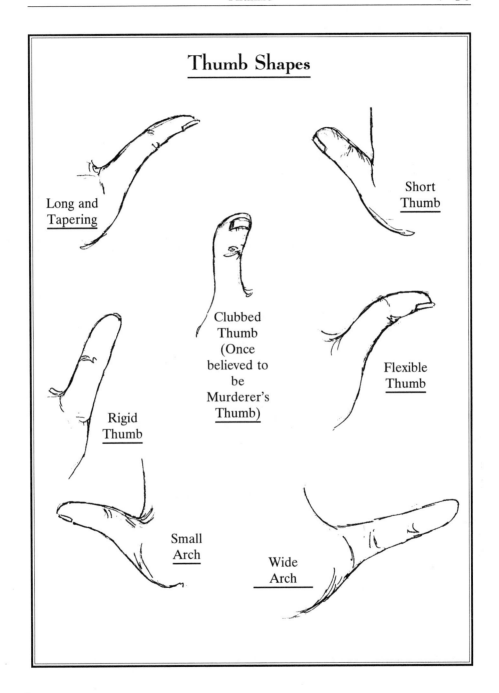

Graphic #21. *A variety of thumb shapes.*

High- and low-set thumbs

The difference between high- and low-set thumbs involves personality traits, usually traits that we're born with.

High-set thumbs that appear to stem from about the middle of the mount of Venus (the raised portion of the palm surrounding the thumb) can show stubbornness and, often, shyness. High-set thumbs that are rigid and don't bend back much can indicate low self-esteem. High-set thumbs on a flexible hand indicate strong will power. Because the high-set thumb begins higher up on the mount, it often looks longer than those starting lower down.

People with high-set thumbs more often have Water/conic or Air/philosophic hands; those with Fire/spatulate or Earth/square more often have low-set thumbs. Fire/spatulate or Earth/square hands tend to be squatter and more angular, including the lower portion of the thumb. When the thumb on an Earth/square or Fire/spatulate is high set, characteristics of the high-set thumb are usually intensified. The opposite exists for the Water/conic and Air/philosophic hand, which is longer and smoother, starting at the bottom of the palm near the wrist. It doesn't angle as greatly, thereby setting the thumb higher at its beginning. This is simply in keeping with the idea that if a person's hand veers from what normally would be expected of a certain pattern or shape, it needs to be looked at more closely.

Low-set thumbs begin closer to the wrist and might appear shorter, only because they begin lower down on the hand, and don't reach as far into the second phalange of the index finger as the high-set thumb. People with low-set thumbs usually enjoy being around others, and if the thumb is excessively long, they yearn for the center of attention.

A few thumb shapes

◆ **Rigid thumbs:** Full of strong will. Loyal to friends. Well organized. Often likes isolation. Tends to march to his or her own beat. Practical and realistic, sometimes to a fault.

◆ **Flexible thumbs:** Often gregarious. Open to new ideas. Makes friends easily. Likes to be around people. Extremely flexible, possibly to the point of overlooking his or her own interests.

◆ **Short thumbs:** Cautious, but can be emotional. A blunt thumb means a busybody and quarrelsome; a short and thick thumb indicates an antagonistic personality.

- **Long, tapering thumbs:** Intellectual. Musical. Spiritual. Warm-hearted and thoughtful. Likes his or her own way.

- **Medium-sized thumb:** Most common thumb size. More balance than short or long in spiritual, friendship/love, and intellectual matters. Reins in emotions.

- **Large and thick thumb:** May be materialistic. Can be very independent. Works best on his or her own. If extremely thick, can be base.

- **Clubbed thumb:** Might be overly determined and persistent. Good sometimes, pesky at other times.

The thumb bump

The "philosopher's bump," as it is sometimes called, found on the outside of the lower joint of the thumb, belongs to the avid reader, the continual student, and to those who study religion and metaphysics. A few examples of people with the thumb bump include:

▶ Al Gore, former vice-president

▶ Celine Dion, musician

▶ Indira Gandhi, former prime minister of India

▶ Marianne Williamson, metaphysical author, lecturer

▶ Humphrey Bogart, actor

▶ Liv Tyler, actor

▶ Sean Penn, actor

▶ Hank Azaria, actor

▶ Robin Williams, comedian and actor

▶ Bob Dole, politician

▶ George McGovern, former senator and presidential contender

▶ Leonard Nimoy, actor

Hand shapes and the thumb

Those with Air/philosophic (elongated) palms tend to have longer thumbs than the other three types. Also, women tend to have smaller thumbs than men, even if their overall hands are nearly as large.

CHAPTER 5

INGER NAMES AND SHAPES

The fingers, along with the thumbs, provide instant assessments of individuals. Peoples' fingers and thumbs can be studied while they're watching television or flipping through newspapers and magazines. Each finger offers different types of insight into a person's personality, character, and strengths.

These insights can be found in such overlooked features as the size of individual knuckles or the space between fingers.

Length of the fingers is mostly unimportant, because it's a holdover from prejudices found in classical and ancient palmistry. Consider that one of America's icons and geniuses, Ray Bradbury, author of *The Martian Chronicles* and *Fahrenheit 451*, among dozens of others, was dubbed "Shorty" as a kid because his fingers were so stubby.

What forms the fingers?

Fourteen phalangeal bones account for the four fingers and thumb of each hand, with three phalanges in each finger and two in the thumb. These bones are interconnected by ligaments and anchored to muscles in the hand. From there tendons connect them to muscles in the arms and shoulders. All of this allows a wide range of movement, accounting for the way individuals hold their hands, which, in turn, paves the way for the way the fingers are held.

Additionally, the palm, or metacarpus, is composed of five long metacarpal bones. These, plus the muscles and ligaments, form the shapes of the palm (as discussed in Chapter 3).

Because the length of each finger in comparison to the others can be manipulated by purposefully twisting the base of the fingers, it's helpful to study them when the hand is not posed.

The way the hand is held in its relaxed and normal position determines how far apart the spacing, or arch, is between the different fingers, or between the index finger and the thumb, and how long the fingers are in relation to one another. If the hand is held a certain way, the index finger may be longer than the ring finger. But on another person's hand, the opposite might be true. It takes years of certain brain activity, and individual ways of looking at the world, to determine how we hold those fingers. Because the way the hands are held involves a person's thinking patterns, finger shapes and positions tell the palm reader a great deal.

Finger names

As palmistry spread from India, Persia, China, and other Eastern cultures to Western society, it acquired the trappings of the cultures in which it gained a foothold. Europeans gave mythological names they were familiar with to certain fingers, mounts, and other formations on the hand. Those named markings, though, represent certain characteristics of the gods and goddesses for which they were named. Thus, the index finger became Jupiter, father god in Roman mythology (taken from Zeus in ancient Greek mythology). The boss. The chief of all the rest. So when that finger is excessively long on a person's hand, it provides a clue that says the person might be domineering. That sign can either be added to or diminished, depending on other markings such as grills, mounts or lines that are found on or near the finger Jupiter. These other markings are covered in subsequent chapters.

In the ancient palmistry tradition of linking certain parts of the hands to the names of ancient gods and goddesses, the idea was to show the full range of their reign, which not only exemplified god-like or goddess-like characterization, but the other side: the human, sometimes silly, often licentious, or ludicrous behavior of these archetypal characters.

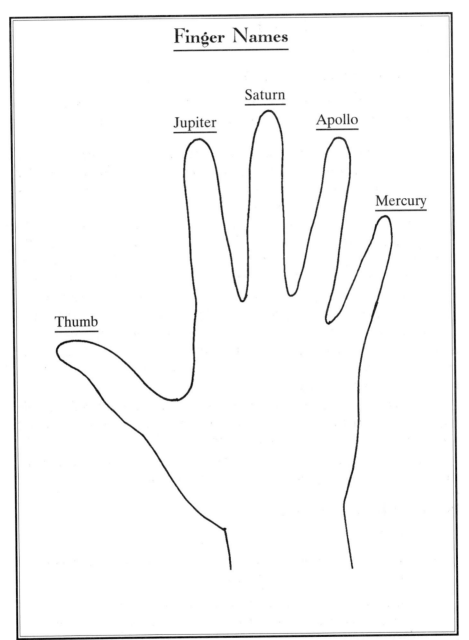

Finger Names

Graphic #22. *Finger names. For purposes of palm reading, each finger takes on the name of a god in the ancient Roman pantheon in Western society. The index finger becomes Jupiter; the middle finger, Saturn; the ring finger, Apollo; and the little finger, Mercury.*

Jupiter (the index finger)

- ▶ Jupiter in Latin.

- ▶ Father or head god of the Roman pantheon.

- ▶ Counterpart in Greek mythology is Zeus, where he was far more licentious and quirky than in Roman mythology.

Because the finger of Jupiter represents the public persona, a well-developed one indicates good self-esteem with the potential for leadership ability, if other markings such as a lengthy line of head, strong thumbs, raised mounts beneath the fingers, or a long little finger, back it up. These additional positive markings, and specific others mentioned throughout the book, simply add to the strength of the long index finger. It can be slightly longer than the ring finger when measured in a relaxed and natural position, but when it is outstandingly long, it means a domineering nature. Napoleon Bonaparte is among historical figures with an excessively long index finger.

It is, however, considered the finger of power and authority and can be a very positive sign if other markings show the person to be a thoughtful and wise leader. The leadership can be within a spiritual community, politics, or a corporation, among others, but with an excessively long Jupiter, financial gain is a driving motivator.

When the index finger is exceptionally short, and as thick as the middle finger, it can indicate people who are more concerned with their outward appearance than having a good inner sense of self.

The investiture rings of bishops, cardinals, and popes are placed on the finger of Jupiter, as if to show the leadership authority.

Saturn (the middle finger)

- ▶ Saturnus in Latin.

- ▶ Roman god associated with agriculture, and also a judge and ruler, especially in the Greek pantheon.

- ▶ Identified with Greek god Cronus (Kronos). The Greeks weren't as uptight as the Romans, so Cronus spread a lot of seed.

- ▶ Also referred to by the Romans as the "digitus infamus" (finger of infamy or bad reputation).

A large, well-shaped Saturn, or middle finger, belongs to individuals with a keen moral, but not necessarily religious, sense. They maintain a strong sense of right and wrong, balance and fairness. Those with this balanced middle finger, which is usually longer and a bit thicker than the others, are often sought by others to help solve problems. They aren't necessarily leaders or bosses, however, in the common vernacular. Rather, they are simply those to whom others turn because they are seen as wise.

As with all the fingers, Saturn can also take on some less desirable characteristics. A middle finger that is a great deal thicker than the other fingers (it naturally tends to be just a little bit thicker than the others), can indicate a melancholy, even depressive, nature.

If the finger is slightly bent inward, the person is overly cautious.

As most of us know, the middle finger also carries some other connotations, which aren't endemic to modern society. Its "giving the bird" origins go back more than 2,500 years to ancient Greece, where at some point it was used during battle to belittle the enemy. Considered a phallic put-down even then, the first written record was by the playwright Aristophanes, who used it as a crude joke.

When Rome imported higher forms of Greek culture, the finger slipped in, too, and became popular enough to earn a few names, such as the digitus infamous or digitus impudicus (impudent finger).

Apollo (the ring finger)

▶ Apollon in Latin.

▶ Associated with music, poetry, and prophecy, as well as representing handsome young men.

▶ Greek mythology reference is Apollon.

▶ Modern-day reference might be "hunk."

The ring finger represents beauty and the arts, and when this finger is nearly as long as Jupiter, it promises creativity and, perhaps, some line of work associated with the arts.

When Apollo is balanced with Jupiter—that is, the two fingers are about the same length when the hand is relaxed—the person has an ability to handle money and personal finances wisely.

If Apollo is exceptionally long, reaching past Jupiter when the hand is held in a relaxed position, a person could have problems developing enough discipline to work the long hours required for success as an artist, despite an abundance of creativity. This same sign (the extra-long Apollo finger) is often found on the hands of compulsive gamblers.

When this finger is excessively thin the individual may feel insufficient to undertake certain endeavors. Excessive thickness, however, belongs to those who love to promote themselves.

Mercury (the little finger)

▶ Mercurius in Latin.

▶ Messenger of the gods.

▶ Also represents eloquence, travel, and cleverness, as well as some association with medicine.

▶ Sometimes linked with thievery.

▶ Becomes Hermes in the Greek pantheon of gods, where he was, at times, a little more daring and mischievous.

A person's little finger, or "pinkie," among other things, tells how adept he or she is at communication and public speaking. When Mercury, the messenger in Roman lore, is long (reaching up to or past the first joint nearest the tip of the finger), it indicates public speaking ability. Politicians, ministers, some teachers, and many actors possess this long little finger.

However, many noted people with shorter little fingers, such as Marlon Brando, Cesar Chavez, and President George W. Bush, have overcome their inhibitions about public speaking, despite their short little fingers, which would indicate a dislike of public speaking. However, because this trait is always there, it will produce times when those with shorter little fingers must use other strengths to force themselves to make public speaking appearances. It becomes even worse if the shorter little finger curls inward toward the palm. Once on stage they might be fine, but getting there could engender the holy terrors.

If the little finger is also thin, it adds to the insecurity and a feeling of vulnerability. When Mercury is excessively long, reaching into the upper phalange (the fingertip) of the ring finger, the person is a limelight natural. Speaking comes nearly as easy to him or her as breathing. A few easy speakers include Jody Powell, former press secretary for Jimmy Carter; Andrew Young, former United States ambassador to the United Nations; and actors Leonardo Di Caprio and Brad Pitt.

A long and fairly thick little finger can mark a person for talent in the fields of economics and finance, business administration, or as a writer, as writing and public speaking ability often go together.

Mercury's association with medicine can be found if the second, or middle, phalange (the one above the knuckle) is much longer than the other two phalanges on either side of it.

Fingertips

Fingertips come in different shapes, adding another dimension to a person. It is usually a good sign to have a hand that combines different shapes than the palm on at least some of the fingers. Thus, an Earth/square palm with a few Water/conic fingertips combines an artistic nature with a hardworking one. Likewise, a Water/conic hand with a few square-tipped fingers offers the conic hand some needed energy to accomplish anything artistically, as most working artists possess an abundance of energy. A Fire/spatulate palm with square-tipped fingers offers the creative nature of the Fire hand some stability.

Different types of fingertips exist to accompany the various types of palm shapes.

▸ Fire/spatulate fingertips: Flare slightly at the top and indicate an energetic, forward-looking, creative nature. These individuals can also be impulsive and aggressive.

▸ Earth/square fingertips: Square and solid-looking at the tip of the finger. Key traits are hard work, loyalty, usefulness, and dependability. They can also be stubborn and bossy.

▸ Water/conic fingertips: Oval-shaped or slightly pointed fingertips. Top traits are a love of the arts, intuitiveness, and a love of finery. Pure conic-handed people can be self-indulgent.

▸ Mixed fingertips: A jack-of-all-trades might have mixed fingertips. Depending on how the person uses the many talents he or she might have, it can be a very successful combination.

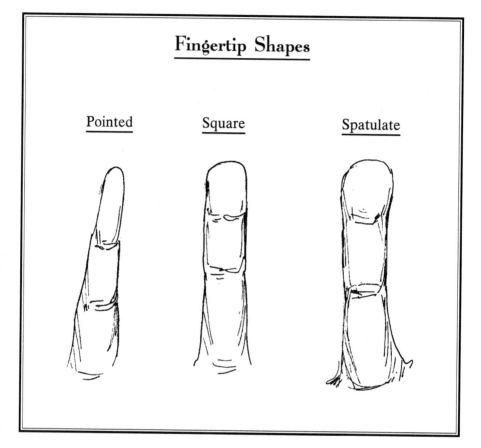

Fingertip Shapes

Pointed   Square   Spatulate

Graphic #23.

Fingertip shapes: Water/conic (artistic, soft energy); Earth/square (solid, dogmatic); and Fire/spatulate (creative, temperamental).

Other characteristics of the fingers

When we really begin examining the fingers, more things come to light than might be expected. We notice things about the hands that we never paid much attention to previously. And although one trait might not seem a good one to have, it's more than made up by other stronger character traits.

Joints

The fingers have three joints, unlike the thumb, which only has two. Two of these joints are in the upper and middle portions of the fingers. The third joint makes up the knuckles. Sometimes the two upper joints are more pronounced, or knobby-looking, rather than smooth, giving a waist-like appearance. Knotty-jointed fingers tend to be on the hands of inquisitive people. These individuals want answers and, when necessary, will dig deeply for them. When I worked as a reporter, nearly all of the investigative reporters I met had knotty-jointed fingers, as well as a good many of those assigned to other beats. Curiosity and obtaining answers and information is just part of a reporter's job.

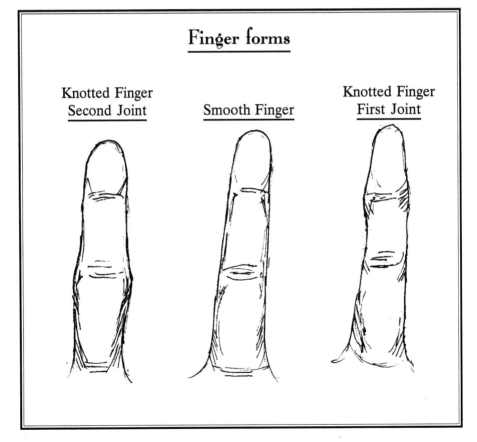

Graphic #24. Finger forms.

Each of these developed joints, though, carries its own meaning. When the upper joint closest to the fingertip is more developed than the middle one, it can indicate a nosey, interfering person, even a gossip. Those with the knotty, or knobby-looking, second joint are analytical, digging types. If either joint or both seem excessively large, it could be a form of arthritis, so it's best to ask.

Smooth-jointed fingers belong to calmer-minded individuals. They are the ones we count on to stay cool under fire.

Knuckles

It might seem improbable, but the prominence of the knuckles also tells us something about an individual. Make a fist, or have the person whose hand you are reading make one, and observe which knuckle is the most prominent. Jupiter and Saturn tend to be the most popular, but the two others also make appearances.

The following are interpretations of what particular prominent knuckles represent:

▶ A prominent Jupiter knuckle stands for strong convictions, dependability, and loyalty.

▶ When a person's Saturn knuckle is the largest, he or she will stand up for his or her beliefs, even in the face of opposition.

▶ Apollo as the largest knuckle shows the person to be materialistic but willing to work hard to maintain that status.

▶ An outstanding Mercury knuckle is a great sign for a public speaker, because it means the person is a gifted orator.

Finger placement

◆ Fingers leaning toward the percussion side of the hand (little finger side) indicate an extroverted nature. The person is emotional and instinctive.

◆ People whose fingers lean toward Saturn (the middle finger) are more serious and take more time to make up their minds.

◆ Fingers that lean toward Jupiter (index finger) signify leadership ability. This is especially so if Jupiter is excessively long. (If this excessively long Jupiter leans toward Saturn, though, it nullifies the leadership ability. Far away from Saturn, and the person wants independence.)

- When Jupiter leans toward the thumb, the person isn't interested in the opinions of others.

- A wide space between the little finger, Mercury, and the ring finger, Apollo, indicates an independent nature.

- A wide space, or arch, between Jupiter and the thumb, shows a gregarious nature that is nonjudgmental and giving.

- Wide spaces between all of the fingers show an extroverted, gregarious person.

- Fingers held closely together signify a shy person.

- Straight fingers that don't bend back easily show a balanced, if somewhat cautious person. When the fingers are excessively rigid, though, the person represses events as a defense mechanism.

- Fingers bending in toward the palm show over-cautiousness.

- Fingers that bend back easily belong to outgoing, giving individuals. If they bend back too easily, the person tends to be gullible and is often taken advantage of. He or she can also be unsure of him- or herself, even though he or she appears outgoing.

Size

- Water/conic hands tend to have medium-length fingers, reflecting their medium-sized hands.

- Earth/square and Fire/spatulate hands generally show shorter fingers, because the palm is more squared, and therefore shorter.

- Air/philosophic hands usually have the longest fingers of all, in keeping with the longer length of the palm.

Phalanges

The basic characteristics of the phalanges take on slightly different meanings on each type of finger. Generally, the first phalange represents intellect, intuition, and reasoning; the second phalange indicates the practical, organizing, and action-oriented capabilities of the person; and the third phalange shows energy, dependability, and loyalty.

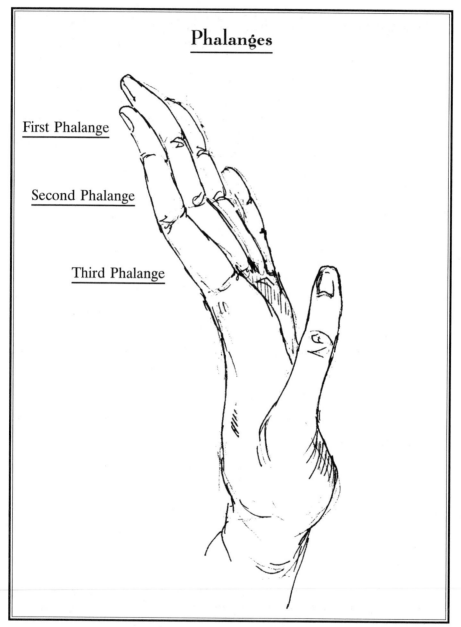

Phalanges

First Phalange

Second Phalange

Third Phalange

Graphic #25.

Phalanges. The first phalange holds the fingertip, the middle section is the second phalange, and the one closest to the palm is the third phalange. They are separated by the joints.

The longest section, or phalange, of each finger is the one that over-shadows the others. They take on different meanings for each finger, as the following information explains.

Jupiter phalanges

♦ If the first phalange is longest, it shows good judgment, often based on intuition. If the finger is thick, it can lead to egotism. If it's thin, the individual is good at controlling others.

♦ If the second phalange is longest, the person is well-balanced in mate-rial possessions, but if the finger is thick, it shows a love of luxury and indolence. When the phalange is very short, energy may be lacking. When that section is thin, it can indicate excess ambition.

♦ If the third phalange is longest, the person has a controlling nature. When it's short, the individuals accept their lot in life. When this sec-tion is thick, it leads to greed; when it's thin it leads to idealism. If the phalange is thick, it adds to the person's controlling nature.

♦ When the third phalange (nearest the palm) narrows the person wor-ries about how others perceive him or her and can be uncertain of whom he or she is.

♦ An excessively thin middle phalange indicates someone who would rather be by him- or herself than to mingle with others.

Saturn phalanges

♦ A long first phalange often signifies a devoutly religious person. It can also lead to superstition, depending on other markings. When the first phalange is short, the person is easily manipulated.

♦ A long second phalange indicates a nurturing person who likes the out-doors, especially gardening. When this phalange is short, the person is distrustful.

♦ The third phalange, if it's the longest of the three, belongs to a loving, sensitive individual. When it's short, it leads to conservatism.

Apollo phalanges

♦ A long first phalange indicates that everything is in place to make a success in the arts. If the first phalange is short, the individual will ignore his or her artistic inclinations.

◆ If the second phalange is longest, the person will be intellectually gifted in the arts. If it's short, creative ideas might be in short supply.

◆ A long third phalange provides the energy to work in the arts. If it's short, not enough energy is available.

Mercury phalanges

◆ As might be expected, when the first phalange is the longest, the person has good communication and intuitive skills. When it's short, the person has difficulty presenting his or her views and can be quite shy.

◆ Aptitudes for medicine and science follow if the second phalange is the longest. Lack of communication skills is evident when the second phalange is short.

◆ When the third phalange is long, it belongs to the natural salesperson who can also manipulate others. When it is short, the person might appear passive, but is extremely honest.

Putting it all together

Now that the shapes of the palms, the fingers, and thumbs have been explained, they can all be put together for some advanced palm reading. Combination hands with a few different types of fingertips usually offer a person more variety and capabilities. (Again, Air/philosophic hands have no specific fingertip types, so they aren't included in the mix.)

◆

Fire/spatulate fingers mixed with:	Indicate people who:
Earth/square palms	Are creative and hard-working.
Air/philosophic palms	Like variety in intellectual pursuits.
Water/conic palms	Are unusual, but extremely artistically creative.
Fire/spatulate palms	Are extreme in all endeavors, with problems finishing multitudes of projects.

Earth/square fingers mixed with:	Indicate people who:
Earth/square palms	Have energy, loyalty, dedication, dogmatism, and an unwillingness to try new things.
Air/philosophic palms	Are hard-working in pursuit of knowledge.
Water/conic palms	Lend energy and dedication to whatever is pursued.
Fire/spatulate palms	Have boundless energy and ideas with constant pursuit of new endeavors.

Water/conic fingers mixed with:	Indicate people who:
Earth/square palms	Possess a love of the arts with the ability to work at new ideas.
Air/philosophic palms	Have strength in classical artistic pursuits.
Water/conic palms	Possess a love of the arts but lack the energy and dedication to pursue an artistic career; also possess a love of luxury.
Fire/spatulate palms	Are unusual but offer intuitive powers and fiery devotion to pursuits.

Phalanges

Generally, the tips of the fingers, or first phalanges, reflect the mental side of the individual and the lower or third phalanges represent the physical nature. Another finding is that a puffy third phalange, whether long or short, indicates allergies to certain foods. The middle, or second, phalange has more to do with practical matters. The longest phalange of the three on an individual's finger determines which is the dominant characteristic.

The specific characteristics work in tandem with the general meaning bestowed on that particular finger, such as the finger of Mercury representing business and sciences; Apollo, the arts; Saturn, mood; and Jupiter, leadership abilities.

First phalange (tips of fingers)

▶ A longer first phalange on the finger of Jupiter belongs to an emotional and sensitive individual. Depending on other markings, the sensitivity can lend itself to charisma as a leader, to psychic abilities, or, at the other end of the spectrum, to uncertainty in decision-making.

▶ If the long phalange is found on the finger of Saturn, it adds to the individual's isolationist cravings. Carried to the extreme it can mean withdrawal from friends and family. If the finger itself tends to be extremely long, or thick, the person can become extremely depressed.

▶ The long first phalange on the finger of Apollo heralds the creative individual. If other markings are positive, such as a line of Apollo (see Chapter 8), it can mean success in the arts.

▶ When the little finger, Mercury, is longest in the first phalange, the person has a bent toward the healing arts, mathematics, or other related sciences.

Second phalange (middle)

▶ A long middle phalange on the finger of Jupiter indicates a reliable, loyal, and articulate person who operates best when working for others.

▶ Any individual with the lengthiest portion on the second phalange of Saturn prefers to work alone—and usually for him- or herself. He or she struggles with a corporate atmosphere and is willing to work for less in order to be free of constraints.

▶ When the longest portion on Apollo appears in the middle phalange, success could be achieved in the arts, but in a practical way. This type of individual would be a steady performer or designer who prefers stability to taking risks with a career.

▶ On Mercury, the individual with a long middle phalange prefers the practical sciences or business. Banking, international trade, investments, and medical administration are among their forte.

Third phalange (nearest the base of the fingers)

▶ The chief characteristic of the person with the third phalange longest on the finger of Jupiter is economics, sometimes including commercialization. Whatever his or her bent, one of the main goals is to understand the flow of money (and for some, a dedication to making money, at which they often excel).

▶ If the third phalange is longest of the three on the finger of Saturn, it adds to the desire to be left alone. He or she might mistrust others.

▶ When the finger of Apollo carries the third phalange as the longest, it introduces people in show business who may be more glitz than substance, but yet they can be entertaining.

▶ On Mercury, a longer third phalange indicates a person who strives in the medical or business world, but who struggles to reach his or her goals. It doesn't come easy, but he or she may have persistence going in his or her favor.

◆

Fingernails

Although fingernails are dead tissue (actually protein), they offer clues about the health and personal quirks of individuals. The portion of the nail to consider is only that which doesn't go beyond the tip of the finger. Long nails past that point mean little to the palm reader. The width is also considered. Texture, color, and markings on them are also of interest.

Fingernails have four basic shapes: long, short, narrow, and broad (measured only to the tip of the finger and from side to side). More often than not, people with Fire/spatulate and Earth/square hands will have round, spatulate, or square fingernails. Oval-shaped and round nails are more likely found on Water/conic and Air/philosophic hands.

When evaluating the following nail type, the measurement means from the cuticle to the tip of the finger (and not beyond it).

▶ Long-nailed individuals tend to be easy tempered and to place importance on their appearance and surroundings. When the nails are excessively long, however, they might lose contact with reality.

▶ Short-nailed people are, more often than not, curious, assertive, filled with energy, and can be nosy. When the nails are extremely short, the person might lack self-control.

▶ Filbert nails are round at the top but wider at the bottom (spatulate-shaped). They belong to peace-loving individuals who seldom get angry or suffer from stress.

▶ Wide nails belong to people with an overabundance of energy and who are outgoing and like adventure. Extremely wide nails indicate an aggressive person. Nails that are both long and wide indicate creativity, but with a certain amount of stress and restlessness built in.

▶ Oval-shaped nails, which can be among the loveliest looking if they are long, are found on conformists. When the oval is extremely small, however, and not taking up much space on the tip of the finger, it might signal poor health.

▶ Square nails are found on the hands of orderly, neat people.

▶ Full, round nails show a generous spirit when they're large. When small, the person becomes envious or jealous.

▶ Good-sized nails that are wider at the top than the bottom show creativity, akin to their counterparts with spatulate-shaped palms.

Minor markings on the fingernails

◆ Horizontal ridges or indentions across the fingernail from side to side are called Beau lines after Dr. Beau, a French physician who, in 1846, related them to poor circulation and other trauma. Beau lines show when the fingernails start and stop growing, based on when a person has had a serious illness.

◆ Vertical lines, or what are sometimes called "fluted nails," can be a sign of poor digestion, nervousness, or chronic illness.

◆ Pitted nails, which appear to have tiny pinprick indentations, can indicate psoriasis or cirrhosis of the liver.

◆ Nails that are thick and soft can be a sign of lung or congenital heart problems.

◆ Curved, or "hump," nails often indicate problems with the respiratory system or colitis.

◆ Loose fingernails are associated with hyperthyroidism.

◆ What are called "spoon nails," because they sink in the middle, can show nutritional deficiencies and nerve disorders.

◆ White spots on the nails may indicate a zinc deficiency or severe stress.

◆ Bluish nails indicate problems with circulation.

Chapter 6

Major Lines of the Hand

Palm shapes need to be considered when determining the meanings of the major lines of the hand. Earth/square and Fire/spatulate hands tend to have fewer minor lines than Air/philosophic and Water/conic hands. (Minor lines are covered in Chapter 8.) Lines are more clear and uncluttered on Earth/square and Fire/spatulate hands. Lines appear to be longer and to be more abundant on Water/conic and Air/philosophic hands. Also, Water/conic and Air/philosophic hands are usually narrower, giving the appearance of longer lines.

For instance, the line of head, which offers clues to the person's intellectual abilities and persuasions, appears longer on Water/conic and Air/philosophic hands. The same line on the Earth/square or Fire/spatulate hand frequently is shorter but can carry just as much meaning. The three major lines of the hand (although there are many others) are the lines of life, head, and heart. The line of life circles the thumb, the line of heart lies horizontally just beneath the fingers, and the line of head lies horizontal beneath the line of heart. These lines have many beginnings and endings.

The line of fate is also included in this category but, despite its name, is not considered as important or revealing as the other three lines just mentioned.

No one line by itself tells a complete story. Where it begins and ends, how strong it is in comparison to other lines, and what type of hand it is on makes for a more complete evaluation.

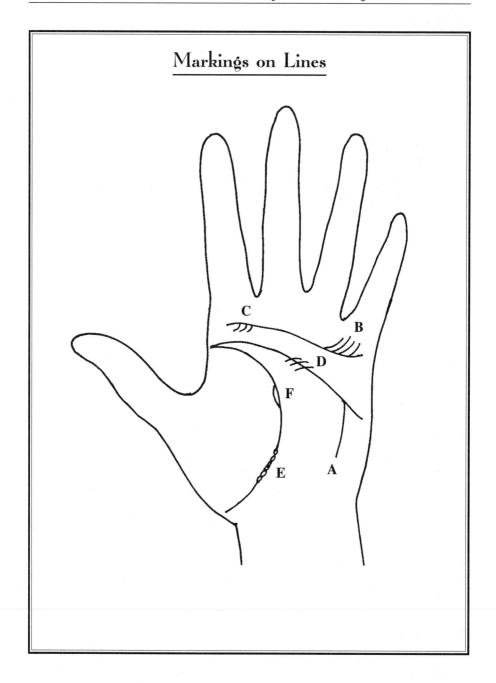

Graphic #26.

Certain markings on lines add additional meanings to major lines.

What forms the lines?

Called "palmar" or "flexion" creases by scientists, the major lines are formed in the womb prior to the 19th week of gestation. The form that the lines take is genetically induced, or produced from environmental conditions in the womb. In addition to the major lines to be discussed in this section, other lines provide a great deal of information about hereditary conditions. These lines are studied by a branch of medical science called "dermatoglyphics." More than one hundred chronic medical conditions have been identified by configurations on the hand by scientists from institutions including Johns Hopkins University School of Medicine and State University of New York at Buffalo.

The lines of life, heart, and head remain pretty much the same throughout an individual's lifetime, although they change color and depth. Many of the minor lines, however (see Chapter 7), change as the person's life is altered by family, work, play, and changing ideas, as well as ways of viewing our inner and outer worlds. Also, new minor lines appear as we grow older. Life is not static. It doesn't always go according to plan. The lines reflect planned and unplanned changes.

Imperfect lines

Seldom do the lines appear smooth, unbroken, deep, and wonderfully colored on people's hands. Most of us have done too much living, planning, attempting, mistake-making, and yearning for any type of perfection to occur. Humans are complicated individuals. We're all unique, but at the same time we're very much alike. And we're all good and bad.

Information about some of the markings that add changes or intrigue to any of the major lines (and some of the minor ones) follows. (Also see Graphic #26 on page 94.)

◆ Forked lines (A). Forks at the termination of lines generally add strength to major lines, such as one branching toward the finger of Mercury and another toward Luna at the end of the line of head, which would signify a vivid imagination, and business acuity.

◆ Small, slanted upright lines attached to major lines (B). These small, feathery lines slanting upwards lend themselves to a few good, or nearly harmless, characteristics. For example, when rising from the line of heart, the lines make the person a natural flirt; when rising on the line of life, they mean continued education.

- ◆ Small, downward-slanted lines attached to major lines (C). Sometimes called "drooping lines," they portray just that. They sap strength from the lines.

- ◆ Frayed lines (D). Feathery lines within the major lines show a loss of energy during the time they appear.

- ◆ Breaks in lines. These breaks in lines show weaknesses or times of illness, especially in the line of life. They are usually backed by parallel lines on either side of the break.

- ◆ Chained formations (E). These chains interrupt the healthy flow of the line, such as the line of life where it might indicate illness.

- ◆ Islands in lines (F). Islands are similar to chained formations, but they are slightly larger, singular, and oval-shaped. They show problems at the time they occur.

The line of life

On the thumb side of the hand, the line of life encircles the mount of Venus, the large mount or pad beneath the thumb. It is more indicative of the energy with which people live their lives, rather than the length of life.

A strong line of life, which begins beneath Jupiter and sweeps out into the palm, ending near the wrist, will be as deep and outstanding as the other two major lines, that of heart and head, both of which lie horizontally above it. When the line begins to fade near its ending, it shows energy dissipating near the end of the life. However, this dissipation is general in meaning, and does not show the age at which this might occur.

Some lines of life stay strong right to the end. The beginning and end of the line of life has many manifestations.

When the line of life ends in a fork, it denotes a restless nature. This individual might like to travel, change jobs frequently, secure many different types of friends or lovers, and attempt new things in work and play. When found on the Fire/spatulate hand, the fork ending adds to the creativity even more so than it does for other hand types. People with this type of hand can go into overload with emotional ideas and be unable to complete projects.

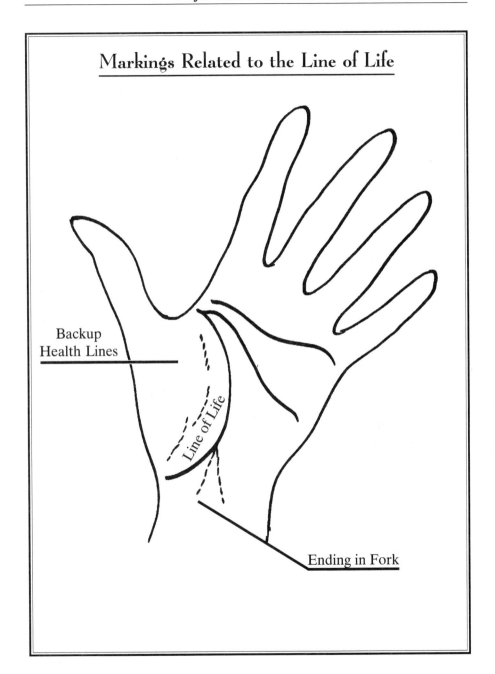

Graphic #27.

Markings related to the line of life.

Other manifestations of the line of life

♦ When an unbroken and unmarked line originates high on Jupiter near the beginning of the finger, the person's energy is solid from childhood.

♦ If the line at its beginning shows breaks, feather lines, chains, or islands, the person may have endured a sickly childhood, which was overcome as the line becomes stronger. If the line, though, shows chains, breaks, or islands as it travels down the palm, it means the individual must guard his or her health throughout life.

♦ A line of life attached at its beginning to the line of head, which lies horizontally just above it, shows an intelligent but cautious person who doesn't like to take risks. They tend to also be very methodical.

♦ When the lines of life, head, and heart (which lies horizontally above the line of head) are all joined together at the beginning beneath Jupiter, the person has a contentious, surly nature and loves a good argument (but rarely listens to the other person).

♦ When the line of life is separated entirely from any other line, with a space between it and the line of head, the person is a risk-taker in life. When this separation is from a quarter of an inch to little under a half-inch (as measured in the uppermost part just beneath Jupiter), the person takes risks in business. This is the hand of an entrepreneur, a person with ideas. He or she would become bored working for someone else. If the separation is greater than a half-inch, the person incorporates other types of risks, maybe involving sports such as bungee jumping. (See Graphics #28 and #29 for examples of touching and separated lines of life.)

♦ Small lines rising from the outside of the line of life, but not cutting through it, are positive marks. When they head toward Jupiter (A), promotions or continued education is a possibility. When they head toward Apollo (B), success in the arts is indicated. When they head toward Mercury, money is promised (C). (See Graphic #30.)

♦ Small horizontal lines that cut through the line of life at any point indicate interference from others. When the horizontal lines aim for the line of fate, which runs vertically from the wrist toward the middle finger, it portends interference in business (D); when it cuts through and touches the line of head (E), someone will interfere with the person's ideas; and when it cuts through and touches the line of heart, it means problems in the love life (F). (See graphic #30.)

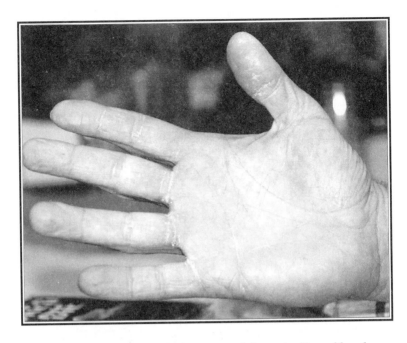

Graphic #28. *The line of life separated from the line of head.*

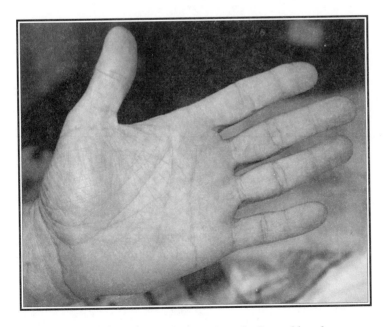

Graphic #29. *The line of life joined to the line of head.*

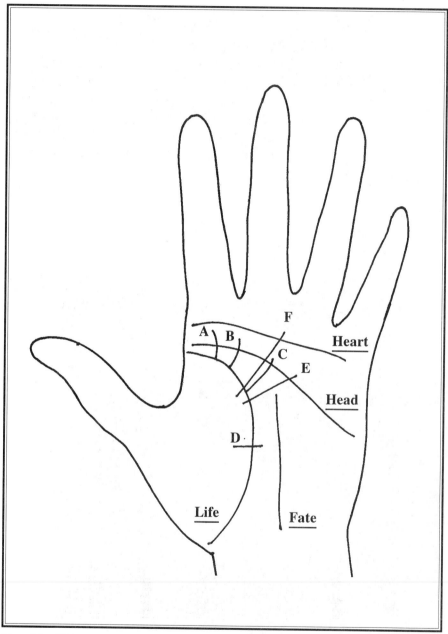

Graphic #30.

The lines of life, head, heart, and fate. Also shown are lines cutting through the line of life and those stemming from it.

The line of heart

The line of heart is the deep line running horizontally across the hand closest to the fingers. It usually begins on the percussion (little finger) side of the hand and terminates on or near Jupiter or beneath Saturn (the middle finger). It is also not unusual for it to fork at the termination point.

A clear, strong line indicates a person who is balanced, nurturing, and caring in relationships with family, friends, and partners. The line should not overwhelm, in depth or color, the line of head just beneath it. If it does, it shows that the heart rules the head.

Graphic #31.

This hand of a Native American healer and visionary is a good example of a strong line of heart, coupled with a strong line of head. It shows good balance.

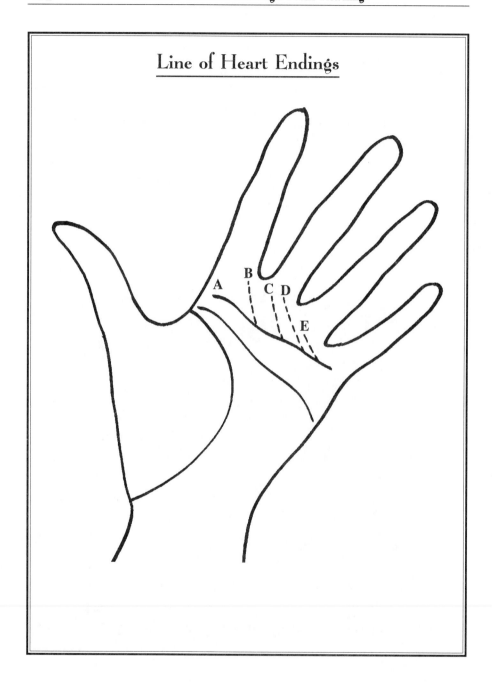

Graphic #32.

Endings for the line of heart.

Endings

Although the line of heart most often ends near Saturn or Jupiter, it encompasses many ending points, each with its own meaning. Note the letters corresponding to Graphic #32.

▶ The line ending beneath Jupiter (A) makes a person idealistic in his or her romantic involvements.

▶ If the line swings upwards and terminates in the finger of Jupiter (B), the person is demanding of others, whether it be romantic relationships or in business.

▶ If the line ends between Saturn and Jupiter (C), the individual is not demanding of a partner but is loving and honest.

▶ When the line of heart ends beneath Saturn (D), the person can be loving but is not demonstrative.

▶ If the line is quite short and ends on or near Apollo (E), the person lacks affection for others.

Other line-of-heart markings

In addition to the beginnings and endings, other markings offer insight into an individual's line of heart. Here are some examples:

◆ When the line of heart sits high on the palm, close to the base of the fingers, the person is intelligent in matters of the heart and makes good choices.

◆ If the line is lower down, close to the line of head, the individual is cautious, possibly due to earlier relationships that caused grief.

◆ A pink-toned line indicates vitality in relationships, with colorless lines showing lack of energy and zest, although the colors can be temporary.

◆ When the line is pale and broad the person isn't inclined toward romantic attachments.

◆ A chained line indicates emotional difficulties dealing with relationships.

◆ Dark spots on the line show melancholy and a sometimes-depressive nature.

◆ Forked lines at the termination points mean the person will be torn between independence and forming deep relationships.

- Small lines that spring upwards from the line of heart show the person to be a flirt.

- Small lines drooping from the line of heart indicate a distrustful nature, possibly brought about by being hurt through romance.

- Breaks in the line literally show heartbreak.

The line of head

The line of head, which lies horizontally beneath the line of heart, is the barometer of the person's mental bent. If it appears to be far deeper and stronger looking than the line of heart, then the head will rule the heart.

For purposes of palm reading, the line of heart begins on the thumb side of the hand just above or touching the line of life beneath the finger of Jupiter.

A long line of head, especially on an Earth/square or Fire/spatulate hand, shows mental ability and agility. Although it is generally longer on a Water/conic and Air/philosophic hand, a line of head that sweeps to the other side of the hand still shows an extremely keen mind and ability. Depending on where this line terminates, it can show where the focus of the person's mental abilities are strongest. (Note the letters corresponding to Graphic #33.)

Beginnings

When the line of head is separated from the line of life, as mentioned previously in the section on the line of life, some further characteristics include an independent and self-confidant nature (A), unless the space is extremely wide. When it is extremely wide (that is, nearly a half-inch), the person can be rash in judgments and projects undertaken (D).

These characteristics—the independent nature, and sometimes the rashness—are usually evident from childhood, often resulting in misunderstandings between parents and children. They simply don't see eye-to-eye until later in life, when more understanding by the parties involved takes place.

When the line of head runs into the line of life, which is the most common placement (B), it indicates a more cautious, rational, and logical nature from the beginning.

Sometimes, one hand will show the line attached to the line of life, and it will be separated on the other hand. If it is separated on the dominant hand, it means that the person has outgrown an inborn trait to be overly

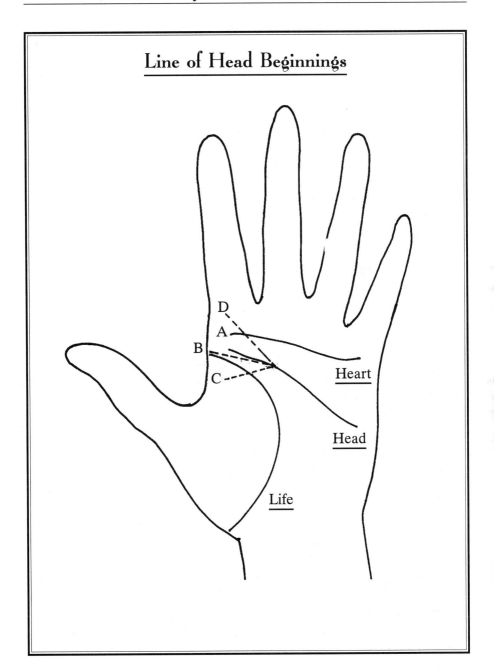

Line of Head Beginnings

Heart

Head

Life

Graphic #33.

Beginnings of the line of head.

cautious and afraid to take risks. When it's reversed (that is, with the separation on the non-dominant hand, or birth, hand), it often means that the person has developed a more cautious nature following traumatic events or failures early in life.

If the line of head crosses the line of life more deeply and heads toward the arch between the thumb and Jupiter (C), it tells of a quarrelsome nature. Individuals with this marking are frequently oversensitive, inquisitive, and can be overbearing.

This one line alone, however, does not doom a person to risk-taking, to rational thinking, or to be overbearing. All other markings must be combined for the full story. What might seem a fault in one situation can be of benefit in another. Maybe the person with the line running into the arch is an investigative reporter who nettles people, but gets the news. Perhaps the risk-taker becomes wealthy from taking chances on a project. And the logically minded person might solve a problem that makes life better for all of humanity.

Endings

The beginnings of the line of head just discussed deal with the outward characteristics and personality of people; the endings show their inward direction. Note the letters corresponding to Graphic #34.

Angling downward toward the mount of Luna, which lies on the percussion (little finger) side of the hand opposite Venus (A), the line takes on helpful imaginative qualities. Many creative types have lines that angle downward or that end with one part of a fork heading toward Luna.

When it angles too drastically (D), the person's imagination runs rampant, often resulting in severe depression or depressive illnesses. The excessively sloping line is frequently a hereditary characteristic, and the person receiving the reading will discuss a parent or other family member who suffered from chronic depression.

When the line is more level and traveling toward Mercury (B), the person is usually endowed with science and/or mathematical ability, as the two often go together. A level line can also indicate someone who is adept in the financial and business world, depending on other corroborating markings on the hand.

If the line curves up slightly as if to head toward Apollo (C), or sends a branch there, it indicates talent in the arts, again depending on other markings that back up the inherent talent.

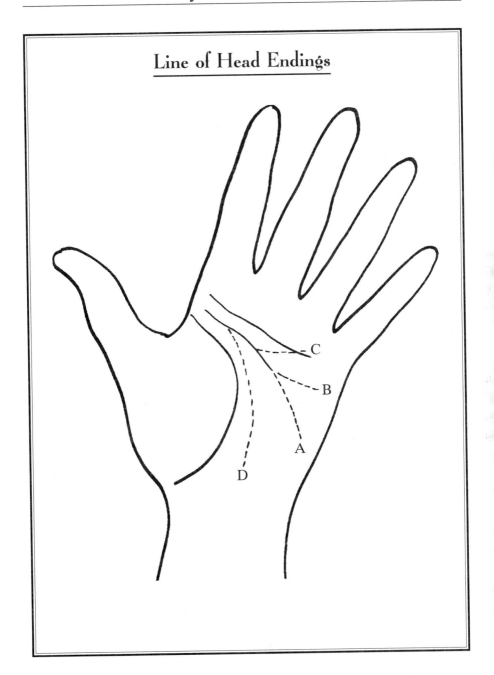

Line of Head Endings

Graphic #34.

Endings for the line of head.

Ending in a fork

When this line ends in a fork, regardless of where it heads, it adds strength to the line, and portends multiple talents, depending on where the forks head.

If a lower fork on a fairly straight line of head veers toward and enters the mount of Luna, it can show talent in two areas, such as business and writing abilities.

The fork also has another meaning: The longest portion of the fork shows which parent the person most likely takes after the most. On a woman's hand, the lower fork represents the father, and the upper, the mother. Thus, if the lower fork is longest, the woman has more of her father's characteristics than the mother's. It's reversed on a man's hand, with the upper fork representing the father, and the lower fork, the mother.

Unique features of the line of head

◆ A short line of head indicates materialism.

◆ Poor memory is shown by a broken line of head.

◆ A weak-looking line means the person has trouble concentrating.

◆ Breaks in the line show traumatic events that disrupt the person's working and career plans.

◆ People with double lines of head are both intellectually gifted and intuitive.

◆ Spots on the line of head beneath Apollo may signify problems with the eyes in old age.

◆ A narrow space between the lines of head and heart is the sign of an introvert; a wide space indicates an extrovert.

◆ A broad line of head indicates an active and physical approach to life. A thinner line denotes a mental approach.

◆ At the beginning of the line, one branch of a fork heading toward Jupiter shows leadership and decision-making abilities.

◆ If the line of head runs straight across the hand but is short, the person is stubborn.

◆ A chained line indicates that a person has problems making decisions.

Combined head and heart lines

A singular line, seeming to combine the head and heart lines, running horizontally across the palm and called the "simian line," has been used for years by medical professionals to check the hands of newborns suspected of Down's syndrome. In another instance, if the singular line is very short, it can mean learning disabilities, but not Down's syndrome.

Another manifestation, not associated with Down's syndrome or learning disabilities but affecting approximately 3 to 5 percent of the population, runs across the breadth of the hand and signals emotional and intellectual intensity. People with this line (sometimes referred to as the "Sydney line") are often quite brilliant in certain areas of their lives, but have problems with relationships. They can become so focused on their areas of interest that little else matters to them once they begin a project.

Once when I pointed out the simian line and its meaning to an architect, he acknowledged that his soon-to-be ex-wife had said the same thing: that when he became involved in projects, he ignored any semblance of family life for days and weeks at a time. He also acknowledged that he ignored everything else when he was involved with his work, and he was perplexed about why he was this way.

People with this combined line of head and heart can be loving, demonstrative, caring, and thoughtful, but they tend to overly center on one object, whether it be work, a hobby, or even someone they love—which can present a different type of problem, because they might be overbearing with the other person. If the individual has a religious bent, he or she might become a fanatic. It can, in other words, be a line of excess or great accomplishment.

Math giftedness and musical ability are often linked to the simian line. It is frequently accompanied by deep, irregular ridge markings on the mounts of the palms and the fingertips.

On rare occasions, the singular line will appear on only one hand, with the other containing the usual lines of head and heart. When it appears on the non-dominant hand it doesn't weigh as much on the personality as when it appears on the dominant hand, because the person is guided by it in the present. That is, an individual's dominant hand reveals the person's present state. (For more information, refer back to Chapter 2.)

The line of fate

Calling this the line of fate may be a misnomer, because it doesn't set the career and personal life in cement. Rather, it offers choices. Depending on where this line begins and ends, it presents insight into the career directions available to the person.

The line of fate, which runs vertically on the palm, rarely runs straight up the hand from the wrist, which is the most common beginning point. Rather, it sprouts from many different locations and sends branches to other locations. It chronicles where individuals have been and where they might be headed. More importantly, it sheds light on the person's potential.

The same as with the other lines and markings, the line of fate needs to be read in context of the other lines and markings. For instance, if the line of fate heads toward Apollo, which is considered the artistic finger, it might portend a career in the arts if the finger of Apollo looks strong, if the line of head dips slightly toward the mount of Luna across from Venus on the percussion side of the palm, and if the mount beneath Apollo is well developed.

The line of fate has several beginnings and endings, each with different meanings. When these beginnings, endings, breaks, and branches are all taken into consideration, a picture emerges of what type of work certain people are suited for, what they are likely to do (which can be different than what they are suited for), when the work will commence or change, and what strengths and weaknesses they bring to the job.

Some people find the right niche early in life; others don't find enjoyable work until midlife or even later. Circumstances often dictate a person's work life, and all people aren't able to "follow their bliss." Many types of work exist, and it's the job of the palm reader to simply try to show the potential outlets for a particular person's talents. And if it's evident that the person has more talent and potential than is being used, make note of it. Discovering a person's potential, talents, joys, and life patterns is more important to a palm reader than predicting the future or rehashing the past, although it inadvertently touches on those issues.

Beginnings

The line of fate is referred by some as the line of Saturn, because its most natural position is heading from the middle of the wrist toward the middle finger (D). Along its path, however, it can send branches in several directions. And it can also begin from other locations.

The line of fate is one of the most changeable of the major lines. I've seen it change dramatically from year to year in people's hands as they try new types of work, add other elements to businesses already established, or reach out for new ways of doing things.

Not all even possess a line of fate. Usually, I've found the lack of one to be on the hands of people who are less in control of their own lives and who are more comfortable allowing others to direct them. Several years ago I read the hand of a woman who had no line of fate, had been married at the age of 16, and had had four children by the time she was 21. In her early 30s, and having never worked outside the home (obviously, she was plenty busy raising four children), she was forced to go to work when her husband was killed in an untimely accident. She had an extraordinary gift for connecting with people and was a hard worker, so she advanced rapidly at the company where she worked, and along the way she developed a line of fate, which she proudly showed me when we met a few years later.

As if going backward, a common location from where the line of fate can emerge is from the line of head, heading downward toward the wrist (A). This is frequently found on the hands of women, in particular, who begin a career after the age of 35. I find this frequently today in the hands of women who have deferred careers until their children begin school. It's interesting to note that when this marking appears, there's a good chance the woman wants to run her own business from the home.

The line of fate can also begin on the mount of Luna (B), indicating people who are intuitive and tuned into others. It's a good sign for people to possess if they are also strong-minded and strong-willed, because taking on too much of others' problems and troubles can be draining. This is more likely to occur if the line of fate begins well down into the mount of Luna, which indicates people who let others direct their lives.

When the line rises near the wrist and closer to the line of life (C), it indicates that the person is tied to the parents for a longer period of time than most. This is especially true if the closely linked line of fate follows the curve of the line of life nearly halfway up the palm.

Endings

The position for the endings of the line of fate doesn't necessarily have to be linked to the beginning, as shown in Graphic #35. For instance, ending E doesn't necessarily need to begin with B. It could arise from D, or other places shown, and travel toward the mount of Jupiter. Each beginning and ending, though, must be taken into consideration.

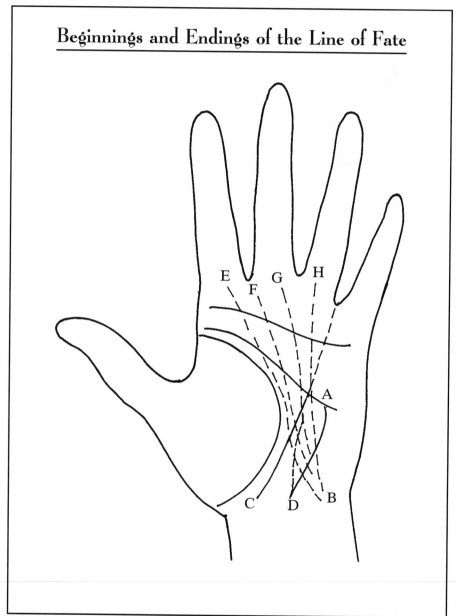

Graphic #35.

Beginnings and endings for the line of fate. The line of fate offers insights into the person's propensities, capabilities, and talents, although talent is not usually inborn, but rather is bred from hard work and persistence, character traits that will also show in the hand.

A line of fate ending on or near the mount of Jupiter (E) indicates leadership abilities. When it runs into the finger, the person possesses a strong desire for power.

If it ends between Apollo and Saturn (F), the pursuits will be in the technical arts, such as architecture, drafting, or surveying.

When the line ends on or near the mount of Saturn (G), the person will be successful in whatever is pursued, because he or she can be assertive and determined. If the line goes into the finger, though, the person may carry things too far. He or she may feel that he or she knows what's best for someone else or even an entire group of people.

When the line of fate travels straight up the palm from the wrist and into the finger of Saturn, it can denote women who have problems letting go of their adult children as well as controlling people.

Ending on Apollo, the line indicates success in the arts. The earlier this line begins, the sooner the individual will achieve success. More often than not, though, success in the arts occurs past the age of 30, and often much later following a different career path. The line of fate can arise from the line of head and end on Apollo, showing a mid-life change of careers, possibly into the arts, if it heads toward Apollo.

Other nuances

Many individuals have more than one line of fate, which can indicate talent in several areas and sometimes more than one career at a time. It can also mean changes in careers. Lines of fate also produce offshoots or branches, which indicate job changes and new careers, depending on where those offshoots and branches head. When studying these offshoots, note the direction in which they head, and use Graphic # 35 to see what area of talent they are using or want to use.

In addition to the branches (or offshoots), other markings affect the reading of the line of head. These include:

▶ Branches from the line of fate indicate career changes.

▶ Branches heading toward Mercury mean financial success.

▶ Branches toward Apollo show success in the arts or combining art into the present type of work.

▶ Branches aimed toward Jupiter indicate leadership positions.

▶ Breaks in the major line indicate setbacks in plans.

▶ Islands on the line show disruptions in plans.

▶ Squares on the line mean preservation from adverse career decisions.

▶ A line of fate closely connected to the line of life indicates an unusual closeness to one's parents into adulthood.

▶ A wide space between the lines of fate and life indicates early separation from the parents. Often further up the line of life, the space will narrow, meaning that the person will make peace with the parents at a later age.

▶ The line of fate is usually stronger (deeper and more clear) on Water/conic and Air/philosophic hands than Fire/spatulate or Earth/square hands.

▶ When the line of fate arises on the mount of Mercury (beneath the little finger), success and happiness come late, following a troubled life.

CHAPTER 7

PALM MOUNTS

I love a hand that meets my own with a grasp
that causes some sensation.

—Frances S. Osgood,
19th-century American poet

The mounts were named after Roman gods and goddesses, which origi-nated with the Greeks under different names.

The mount that corresponds to each finger shares its name with that finger. In other words, the mount beneath the index finger becomes Jupi-ter; beneath the middle finger, Saturn; Apollo, who kept his Greek name, sits beneath the ring finger; and the mount of Mercury, linked to trading and profit, takes over for the little finger. Mars, who was originally an agri-cultural god, and later became the Romans' god of war, finds two places on the palm, as the mounts of upper Mars and lower Mars.

The three mounts on the palm side of the hands are found beneath the fingers on the percussion side of the hand encompassing the area beneath the little finger, another area just below that called upper Mars, and fur-ther down encompassing the lower half of the percussion side of the palm called the mount of Luna.

The thumb side of the hand has two mounts: the mount of lower Mars, situated between the thumb and finger of Jupiter, and Venus, the large por-tion surrounding the thumb. Two other minor mounts, Pluto and Neptune, have places closer to the wrist on the palm. Pluto is near the wrist, beneath the little finger, and Neptune is near the wrist in the middle of the palm. (These mounts can be seen in Graphic #36.)

The fingertips are the most noted mounts or pads on the hands; they were recognized and used scientifically for many years before any of the other mounts fell under scrutiny. The others, however, now involve serious research by medical scientists, because the dermal ridges, among other markings, provide clues about congenital health conditions.

Because the mounts are linked to energy, each mount offers several types of information.

The mounts are usually better developed on Air/philosophic and Water/conic hands than on Fire/spatulate or Earth/square hands. That's because Water/conic and Air/philosophic hands are naturally fleshier than Fire/spatulate or Earth/square hands, which are naturally flatter and more firm. That's also why pads on square and spatulate palms are more significant.

The two major mounts of the hand

The mounts of Venus and Luna lie across from one another. When both are well developed, a person is promised passion and energy, coupled with a good imagination.

The mount of Venus

Venus, one of the most noted and largest mounts, lies beneath the thumb and is also associated with Aphrodite, the Greek goddess of love and beauty. Although the names represented different cultures, the goddesses have similar attributes. In turn, Aphrodite's origins are thought to be oriental, with greater meaning toward sexual desire than Venus. Aphrodite, often portrayed as nimble and soft, also achieved a reputation for being destructive toward men.

Venus, as with many of the mythical goddesses of ancient lore, could represent either the spiritual or pure sensual side of a person. On the palm, the mount of Venus means the same thing on both male and female hands.

Passion, though, can mean anything from a love for the arts to sex, or both. When people feel good about themselves, are involved in physical as well as mental activities, and maintain interests in things outside themselves, they tend to be more "passionate" about different types of activities. This energy and passion spill over into everyday life and shows on the hands.

Mounts

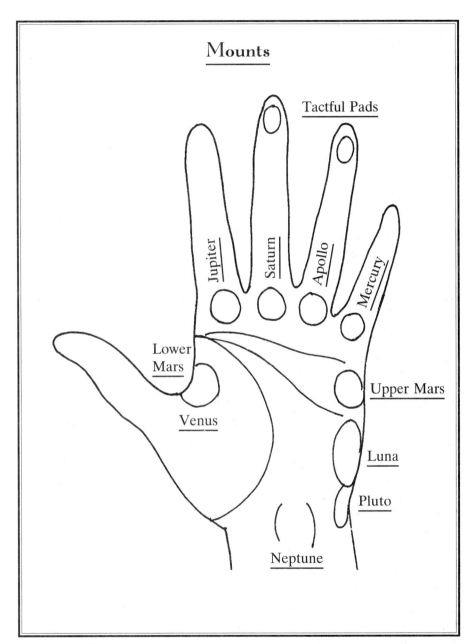

Tactful Pads

Jupiter

Saturn

Apollo

Mercury

Lower Mars

Venus

Upper Mars

Luna

Pluto

Neptune

Graphic #36.

The mounts should be fairly firm and elastic to the touch to show the highest energy. Because a person's energy is changeable, the pads will be more robust when the person is feeling full of zest and passion.

When Venus is well padded and elastic to the touch, but not abnormally large, although it is usually puffier than the other mounts, it shows good energy and passion. The line of life surrounding this mount should also circle well out into the palm in the lower portion of the mount. When the arch is narrow, people can be energetic, but lacking in passion or overly cautious.

If the mount is soft and flabby (rather than elastic), as well as puffy, the individual's sensual nature is out of control.

At its best, the mount represents a warm loving nature, and also energy and passion for living.

The mount of Luna

Luna, lying on the percussion side of hand, was transformed from the Greek goddess Selene (also called Phoebe), who eventually became associated with the moon. The term *lunacy* came from this association. Because she presides over the mount of imagination, this is fitting. Just the right amount of elastic puffiness leads to a well-developed imagination; too much is lunacy.

Luna is also associated with the moon goddess and has at times been worshipped by such various ancient people as Diana, Artemis, and other mythological beings. Some mythologies associate the ancient worship of the moon with women's menstrual cycles.

In addition to imagination, Luna is associated with spirituality, the occult, intuition, and visions. A person with a well-developed mount of Luna may lean toward mysticism and have an ability for abstract reasoning.

When this mount is well developed, and certain lines head in its direction, it signifies creative abilities in the arts. But it's not only for the artist or writer, because it bestows a love of beauty in all endeavors, as well as an appreciation for nature and the capabilities for reverence toward Mother Earth.

A well-developed mount of Luna also offers the person a good sense of self and even a bit of egocentricity.

If the mount is excessively developed, however, and lines, such as the line of head, run into it, nearly reaching the wrist, the imagination will run rampant, leading to obsessions with the very qualities that make it unique. People become religious fanatics or obsessed with their beliefs about the environment or loved ones.

In other words, this is a strong mount that can offer men and women much beauty and creativity—or trappings of the beast.

The mounts of the fingers

Each mount lying beneath, or in between, the fingers produces special meanings. When it lies directly beneath the finger, it takes on the meaning of that finger. When it lies between two fingers, it often combines the meaning of both fingers on either side of it. In other words, if a mount lies between the ring finger and the middle finger, the person could be both artistic and somber, preferring more serious themes in art or music. Overlapping mounts have combined meanings of the two fingers.

The mount of Mercury

When the mount of Mercury is well developed, it takes on the same meanings as that accorded the little finger as a bearer of luck in financial and mathematical undertakings, speaking ability, the capacity to rebound from emotional traumas, and natural medical skills.

A well-developed mount also indicates a good sense of humor. If it is fullest by the side of the hand, the person is quick to take action when faced with difficulties. If it is puffiest near the line of heart, the person responds well to emergencies.

Those with long little fingers, plus a well-developed mount of Mercury, are affable, are fun to be around, and can be naturally entertaining. They like people.

If the mount is excessively large, the person can be greedy, and prefers to always be the center of attention.

When the mount leans toward Apollo (that is, it lies between Mercury and Apollo), and if other markings are favorable, it promises success in the arts, because Mercury shows good business sense, combined with Apollo, indicating the arts. Additional markings to enhance success in the arts might include a line of Apollo (see Chapter 8) or a line of head that terminates on Luna, the mount of imagination.

The mount of Apollo

Representing the finger of beauty and the arts, a well-developed mount of Apollo lends further capabilities in those areas.

Apollo, also known as the sun god, was associated with poetry, prophecy, music, and medicine in classical Greek mythology. He was identified with Helios, an earlier Greek sun god. Apollo is also the twin of Artemis, of the moon goddess hierarchy.

Often when the mount of Apollo (at the base of the ring finger) is well developed, so is the mount of Luna, which blends the love of the arts with the imagination.

In a twist of events, though, when the mount is overly puffy, it can lead to arrogance and vanity. If it's flat, it belongs to people who struggle with their spirituality.

When the mount is puffiest between the finger of Apollo and that of Saturn, the leanings in the arts may be toward more somber music and writings.

The mount of Saturn

Lying at the base of the middle finger, the mount of Saturn indicates a love of solitude and a lifelong interest in improving the mind. A puffy mount of Saturn indicates a perpetual student, whether it be via formal schooling or self-teaching.

The Roman festival of Saturn took place at about the same time as the Western world's Christmas and other Winter Solstice celebrations, so Saturn is also associated with unrestrained revelry.

The negative side of Saturn occurs when the mount is well developed and the finger is excessively thick or long, as this can indicate moroseness and sluggishness.

When this mount leans toward Jupiter, it combines the meanings of those two mounts, indicating the possibility of a very learned person who wants to be a director or manager but who may lack the interpersonal skills for leadership.

The mount of Jupiter

The mount of Jupiter (at the base of the index finger), deals with an individual's leadership capabilities. It denotes power and authority, much as the god for which it is named commanded from the Romans.

Also called Jove, Jupiter is the counterpart of ancient Greece's Zeus, father of the Greek pantheon of sometimes-squabbling and ribald gods and goddesses. Jupiter, representing knowledge and power, became more straight-laced once adopted into the Roman pantheon.

When the mount represented by Jupiter is well developed, it provides the ability to manage others, strong leadership capabilities, and the proclivity to take tough stands for certain beliefs, while at the same time being aware of the feelings and thoughts of others.

In the extreme, when the mount is excessively developed—and especially if the finger of Jupiter is exceptionally long—the person will turn to bossiness and dominance. Such a person can be a hard taskmaster.

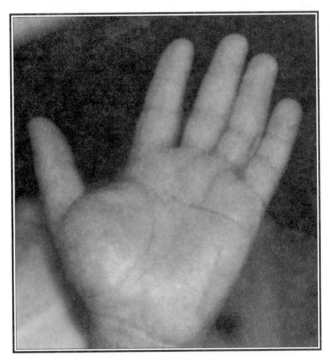

Graphic #37. Mounts.

This hand belongs to a married man who supervises computer technical support, is a gourmet cook, is a patron of the arts, is well read, is interested in a variety of subjects, is an investor, enjoys the outdoors, and is the father of four boys. His hand, with well-developed mounts on all of the fingers, is a good example of an individual who is enjoying the best life has to offer. His palm also shows the beginning of an Old Soul mount, to be discussed later in this chapter.

The minor (lesser) mounts

The lesser mounts can help round out a person's initial personality traits and some physical characteristics. The lesser mounts tell us about pain thresholds, allergies, stubbornness, fighting spirits, and wisdom, among other things.

The mount of lower Mars

Some mounts, such as lower Mars, found in the arch between Jupiter and the thumb and lying close to the line of life, can be interpreted two ways. Most important, when it is puffy, it indicates a person who can withstand a great deal of physical pain. Many prizefighters and other athletes have this mount well developed. But I've also found it on the hands of many women who acknowledge that their doctors have remarked about their ability to withstand pain.

Usually the ability to withstand more pain than the average person is an inborn trait, as some people are born with physical and mental makeups that allow them to tolerate pain to a greater degree than others. Lower Mars is far flatter on people who have a low tolerance for pain.

Both high and low tolerances for pain are thought to rely on nerve impulses, generated by a painful stimulus, that encounter a cellular "gate" on their way to the brain's pain center. Whether the gate is open or closed helps to determine the sensation of pain. A person's mood, emotions, beliefs, and thought patterns, as well as the inborn nervous system, can contribute to opening and closing this gate.

After reading palms for years, I've found that many people who are unable to withstand much physical pain are good at handling psychological trauma, whereas many people who have high pain thresholds aren't so good at handling psychological trauma. Also, I've found a raised lower Mars mount on women's and men's hands alike, meaning that women and men can tolerate pain equally well. A great many athletes are able to withstand more physical pain than the norm.

The mount of upper Mars

Found on the percussion side of the hand (the little finger side) and just below the line of heart, a developed upper Mars signifies an assertive nature, given to overcoming obstacles and withstanding hardships. As with the well-developed mount of Venus, when this mount is full and elastic a person is promised energy and enthusiasm for life. A full and elastic mount of upper Mars is also found on the hands of people with good senses of humor.

Upper Mars actually travels down the percussion side of the hand to add fullness at the side of Luna. When it is extremely full in the lower portion of the palm, it means the person has a love of water and related sports.

The mount of Pluto

The mount of Pluto is found slightly lower than the lowest portion of the mount of Luna as it starts to reach the wrist. Pluto actually encompasses part of the side of the upper wrist.

In ancient Roman belief, Pluto ruled the lower world, as did his Greek counterpart, Hades. Because the lower world included buried riches such as gold and silver, Pluto was also associated with wealth, although some mythologists say this was a misnomer. For palmists, the mount of Pluto stands for wisdom. People with developed mounts of Pluto are sought for their advice and often serve as mentors.

The old soul mount

The old soul mount, which is rare, encompasses a portion of the mount of Pluto, but goes on to spread further down into the wrist, engulfing the lower side of the palm into the wrist area. For those who believe that we live many lives, the presence of this mount signifies several incarnations. I've dealt with many people who believe they have lived many lives, but who do not possess this mount. It shows up in the hands of people who are quite surprised by its appearance, such as that of the computer technical support supervisor shown in Graphic # 37. A practicing Catholic, he is not particularly interested in past-life traditions.

The mount of Neptune

The mount of Neptune lies just above the wrist bracelets on the palm side of the hand between Venus and Luna, the center of the lowest portion of the palm. Neptune, to the Romans, was the Greek counterpart of Poseidon, second only to Zeus in the Greek hierarchy, because their culture was so closely tied to the sea. Although he was ruler of the sea, and therefore a powerful force, he was also noted for providing the first horse to man.

In classical palmistry, a developed Neptune, which actually joins Luna and Venus as one raised portion near the wrist bracelets, bestows vitality, passion, imaginative powers, and endurance.

Tactful pads

On the inside of the fingertips, some people's hands contain small extra pads on a few or on all of the fingertips. People with these pads, sometimes called "sensitivity pads," are extra-sensitive to the feelings of others. They will go out of their way to keep from hurting someone's feelings. If used correctly, this is a positive trait, because the person is more diplomatic in stressful or volatile situations. Many top administrators and leaders possess a few tactful pads.

Carried to the other extreme, though, these pads can interfere with decision-making, being truthful, and resolving issues.

The Earth mount

Found on the opposite side of the palm, the Earth mount lies beneath the finger of Jupiter at the arch of the thumb. When pressing the thumb against the area just below Jupiter, it rises and becomes spongy, and sometimes quite hard. This mount shows a person's energy level, which can vary at different times during the day, at the time it is pressed. The harder it is, the more energy and strength and it shows.

CHAPTER 8

MINOR LINES AND

THEIR MEANINGS

The line of Apollo

The line of Apollo (A) runs vertically from the mount of Venus toward the finger of Apollo. (See Graphic #38.) It can also stem from the line of life (B), from the line of fate (C), and from the line of head (D), and end somewhere on the mount of Apollo. Whatever its course, it promises success in the arts. Some people's palms will show the line springing from more than one location. This is not always desirable, because it may scatter the thoughts and ideas among too many areas.

Beginnings

◆ **From Luna to Apollo (A):**
Imaginative artistic work that begins at an early age but comes to fruition with the help of others.

◆ **From the line of life (B):**
Depending on where it stems from on the line, it may show the approximate age at which time the person will pursue artistic interests. (See the Appendix for more information.)

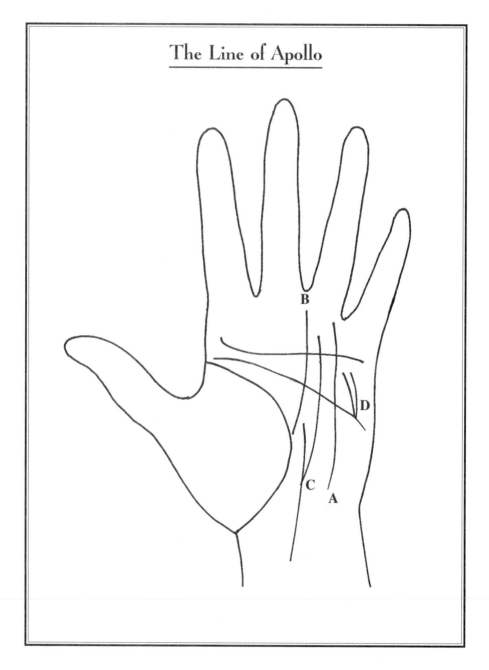

The Line of Apollo

Graphic #38.

The line of Apollo.

◆ **From the line of fate (C):**
Starting from the line of fate, artistic pursuits are often connected to other types of work in which the person is already engaged.

◆ **From the line of head (D):**
When it springs from the line of head with a fork, it promises success after the age of 40 in some artistic endeavor.

Health-related lines

The line of health

The most common position for the line of health is stemming from the mount of Mercury, and heading down toward the line of life (see Graphic #39, A). However, it rarely travels in a straight line, and it rarely reaches the line of life. It can also appear as several smaller lines side by side or as wavy or chained lines. In many cases, it is missing altogether, which to my mind is a favorable sign, because it indicates that no inherited conditions have manifested themselves, and nothing is troubling the system enough to create a line.

The line of health usually represents the condition of the liver and vital organs. The condition and shape of the lines offers clues to a person's health. Note the letters corresponding to Graphic #39. For example:

▶ A red and inflamed line shows toxins in the body. I have seen it reddened repeatedly on the hands of people who smoke cigarettes.

▶ If the line touches or cuts through the line of life (B), the person's health will be compromised at that time. It doesn't necessarily strike a dire warning; it just means that health concerns will be uppermost in the life at that time.

▶ A series of small lines side by side in normal area for the line of health (which runs between the little finger and the middle finger in the upper portion of the hand, toward the lower portion of the line of life) indicates bad digestion (C).

▶ Wavy lines (or a single wavy line) signify eventual problems with the gall bladder or liver (D).

▶ Lines that are chained indicate potential problems with the lungs (E).

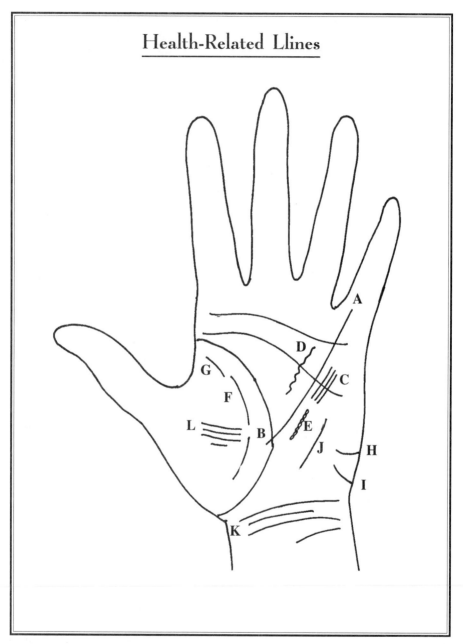

Health-Related Llines

Graphic #39.

Health-related lines.

Lines of health can also fade and disappear, especially if a person decides to begin eliminating bad habits that may be contributing to the condition or decides to receive medical treatment for conditions that compromise the body.

Backup lines

Backup lines of health are fine lines found parallel to, and running inside, the line of life on the mount of Venus. These accompanying lines serve as backup health lines when a break, chain formation, or island appears on the line of life. Sometimes these backup lines do not manifest themselves until a severe illness or disability occurs, especially if these backup lines are nearly as strong as the major line (F). Some people's hands do not contain these backup lines at all. The absence of these lines has nothing to do with hand shape.

Usually when these backup lines are fainter than the major line, the person becomes ill with minor conditions (such as the flu) quite regularly, but he or she bounces back rapidly. People without backup lines, but with one strong line of life running down the palm, become ill infrequently throughout their lives, but when they do it keeps them down for a longer period of time.

The antibody or Mars line

Another backup line, sometimes called the "inner line of life" or the antibody line, the Mars line (G) stems from the lower Mars area. This line increases the person's stamina and adds protection when breaks or islands occur in the line of life.

The allergy line

The allergy line (H) is a small but distinct line that runs horizontally along the base of the mount of Luna near the wrist. People with this line suffer more from pollutants, pollens, and chemicals than most.

Friendship lines

These horizontal lines (L) on the mount of Venus, not touching the line of life, indicate an individual's ability to acquire many friends. Lines that cross the line of life indicate people who interfere in the life of the person whose hand is being read.

The indulgence line

The indulgence line (I) is often confused with the allergy line, because it occurs in the same vicinity, but it curves upward from the wrist bracelets and characterizes a person who overindulges in foods or alcohol/drugs.

The cephalic line (Via Lasciva)

Running next to the line of heath (or near the usual place for the line of health if it is missing)—but far shorter—this line (J) promises good health and passion for life.

Wrist bracelets

Wrist bracelets (K), also known as rascettes, are lines that run horizontally on the wrist. If they are clear and unbroken, it shows excellent health. When they are made up of islands or chains it indicates anxiety. In classical palmistry, at least three unbroken horizontal lines at the wrist promise a long life. However, I've also seen a maze of broken and unsteady lines on the hands of many people past the age of 80. The top wrist bracelet arching into the palm on a woman's hand can mean trouble during childbirth.

Lines related to mental nature

More than a dozen lines provide information about an individual's mental nature (Graphic #40). Few people's hands contain all of these lines, but palmists are likely to find at least one or two of them on a person's hand.

The girdle of Venus

A much fainter line than the major lines of life, head, and heart, the girdle of Venus (A) lies slightly horizontal above the line of heart. It is sometimes seen in two or three parts. People with the girdle of Venus can be unusually bright, entertaining, emotional, and prone to hypochondria. The line also stands for a love of luxury, sensitivity, and, sometimes, sensuality. I've seen it equally on the hands of men and women, interior decorators and also rugged outdoorsmen.

The line of intuition (moon line)

The line of intuition (J) (also known as the moon line) lies, as it should, on the mount of Luna and is a curved and distinct line. It has long been

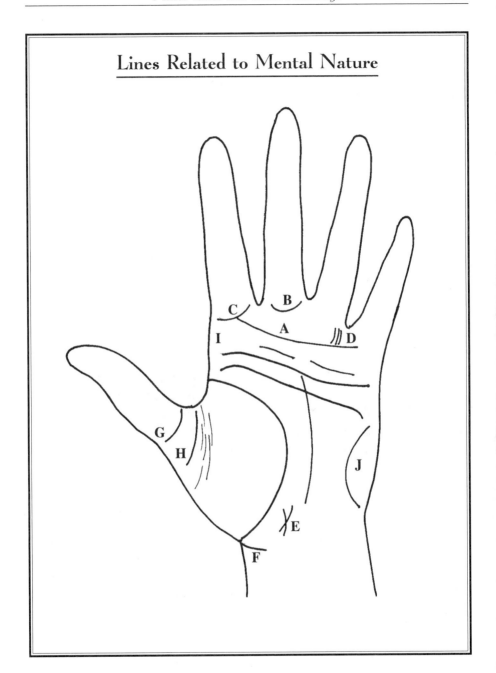

Lines Related to Mental Nature

Graphic #40.

Lines related to mental nature.

associated with people involved in metaphysics and the occult. However, many intuitives, psychics, and metaphysical teachers I've met do not have this curved line. More often, I've seen it in the hands of people who take risks with their beliefs and who follow their own paths.

The ring of Saturn

This small half-ring or eyelash-shaped line (B) beneath the finger of Saturn, which can be a temporary sign, shows a loss of energy and penchant for melancholia, as well as a tendency toward unfinished projects and business.

The ring of Solomon

The ring of Solomon (C), another half-ring, found beneath the finger of Jupiter, can be a very favorable sign, because it belongs to the natural adept, psychic, or metaphysician. Such leanings are inherent to people who possess this line without formal instruction or study. In fact, they often become metaphysical teachers.

Healer's marks

A series of short vertical lines on the mount of Mercury called healer's marks (D) belong to people with natural abilities to help others heal emotionally, physically, and spiritually. Healer's marks can be found on the hands of nurses and others in the healing profession, but I've seen them many times on the hands of people in a variety of professions who simply know how to listen and offer comfort to others free of judgment. These people seem unaware of their abilities but often have a dearth of friends.

St. Andres's Cross

A marking (E) with a meaning similar to that of healer's marks can be found in either the shape of a cross or a small, semi-horizontal line lying between the line of life and the line of fate. It belongs on the hands of those who give aid and are deeply concerned with the welfare of others, often on a global scale.

The escape or avoidance line

This short horizontal line (F) at the bottom of the line of life, which may or may not touch the line of life, belongs on the hands of people who try to escape from life and responsibilities. Often they channel their energies into drugs, alcohol, and other unhealthy habits.

The line of stubbornness

Indicating a stubborn nature, this distinct line (G) is found on the inside of the thumb above the bottom line that separates the thumb from the mount of Venus. Ironically, it sits in the overall area of the phalange that stands for logic. This line can also represent a tenacious, persistent nature.

The temper lines

The temper lines (H) lie just below the line of stubbornness on the thumb and just above the lines that make up the second joint, closest to the mount of Venus. Frequently they are seen with the line of stubbornness, indicating a quick temper.

The curiosity line

A short horizontal line on the mount of Jupiter near the side of the hand, the curiosity line (I) adds to a person's curious nature. If it's channeled in the right direction, such as following through on wanting to find the right answers to a question (as opposed to just being a busybody), the curiosity can provide benefits to the person's life, as he or she tends not to be bored or boring. It is placed further outside than the Ring of Solomon (C), sometimes beginning on the outside of the palm.

Minor lines concerning relationships

Relationship, affection, or marriage lines

It may seem a misnomer to call relationship or marriage lines "minor," but they are so called because relationships (not only love relationships) might be one of the most important human attributes. These lines are so called, though, because they are smaller than most of the other lines in other parts of the hand. Also, they aren't always clear enough for a good reading. (See Graphic #41.)

The lines found at the side of the hand beneath the little finger, and above the line of heart, which usually wrap slightly around the outside of the palm, make up the deep relationship or marriage lines (A). Years ago when reading palms, I nearly always referred to them as marriage lines, but as times changed, and more people began living together without getting married, they became "deep" relationship or marriage lines. By that, I mean that only marriages or relationships that have impacted one's life to any great degree are going to show up there. Other affairs and short-term love relationships may show up as short lines farther down beneath the line of heart on the percussion side of the hand that separates the outside of the hand from the palm (B). These lesser lines can also stand for someone who attracts many friends and acquaintances.

There are no special markings to designate the gender of a love relationship. It can be male/female, female/ female, or male/male. All of these types of relationships deal with the same issues that affect all couples.

Despite their short length, relationship/marriage lines provide a great deal of information by their length, color, depth, and other markings. Also, these other markings can change, depending on the status of the relationship at the time of the reading.

Notes on relationship lines

◆ Strong, deep, pink-tinged lines stand for lasting, solid relationships.

◆ Deep, red lines can show active anger at the time of the reading.

◆ A line with an island in it indicates a separation from the partner.

◆ A short vertical line that cuts the relationship line stands for interference from a relative.

◆ A line that ends in a fork or breaks in the middle might indicate a split-up.

◆ Even with other lines present, the strongest, and usually the longest, line indicates that one particular relationship stands out from the rest as the most meaningful.

◆ Shorter, fainter lines show a lack of commitment.

◆ Lines that are puffy around the edges show turmoil going on in the relationship at the time of the reading.

◆ Lines that curve upward, or send a branch upward, can mean that unless the person is joined with someone who makes few demands, he or she might feel stifled within a marriage. It doesn't, however, mean the individual isn't loving and caring.

◆ Little hairlines drooping from the line indicate a good chance that the person's partner will be ill frequently.

◆ A faint line running close and parallel to the relationship line can indicate that the person will have an affair during the marriage.

Relationship Lines

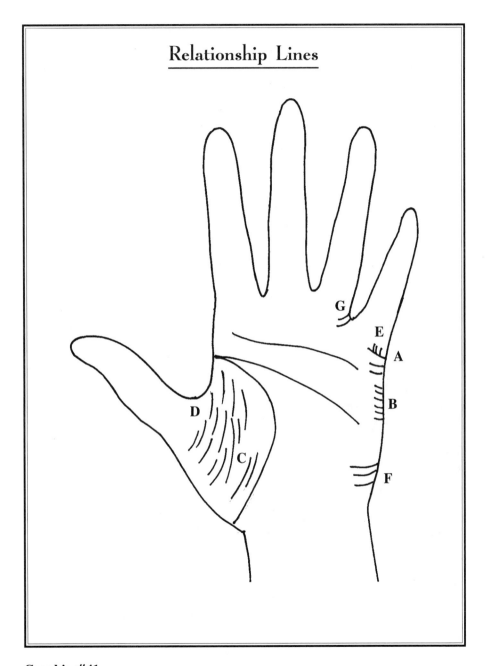

Graphic #41.

Relationship lines.

♦ Backup lines on the mount of Venus (C) portend an exceptionally strong union. These lines shouldn't be confused with backup health lines. If there is a break in the line of life at the same position as what could be a backup marriage line, the health lines take precedence. Also, other curving lines found on the mount of Venus (D) signify someone who attracts numbers of people to them, both as lovers and friends.

Another point worth noting is that when I first began reading palms nearly 30 years ago, the first questions people asked me (after concern with the length of the line of life) were usually about the status of a marriage, affair, or upcoming or potential relationships.

Today, questions concerning relationships run neck-and-neck with those about careers and career changes. People also ask more questions than ever before about health issues. All of these concerns seem to me to revolve around relationships—not just love relationships, but about how a person deals with and responds to other people. Having good relationships with others helps to foster physical and mental well-being and boosts careers.

A career consultant/psychologist I once interviewed said that parents who encourage their children to develop good people skills do them more of a favor than when they just push them toward prestigious careers by hounding them about school work, obtaining an education, and making a lot of money.

Children lines and their backup lines

The first thing to look for lines of existing children, or children indicated in the future, are short upward lines sprouting from the relationship line or marriage line (E). Because years of birth are not indicated on a parent's hand, children needn't be born to indicate that children will be part of the relationship or marriage. Often the lines are too faint or confusing to isolate, very rarely being as clearly marked as they are in Graphic #41. Sometimes, though, they stand out as clear as a bell's chime. The very straight short lines stand for boys, and the slightly bending ones indicate girls.

If the lines are faint, and the reader isn't certain about them, they can be double checked with those that sometimes appear as horizontal backup lines on Luna just up from the wrist (F). These backup lines usually start at the back side of the hand and wrap into the mount. Most often, they are found on the hands of mothers, but in recent years I have seen more of them on the hands of fathers. When they're found on a man's hand, it is usually an indication of someone who is exceptionally close to his children. The lines show because they are uppermost in an individual's mind. Sometimes one of the backup lines, or one of the original children's lines on the marriage line, will appear deeper or be slightly red (or have some other outstanding trait). This generally means that one particular child is uppermost in the parent's mind at the time of the reading, usually due to a bit of trouble or other concern.

When the lines don't show as clearly in either place on the hands of individuals, it doesn't mean they are less caring about their children. When they do show, it's a bonus.

Inheritance lines

Lines of inheritance (G) appear in the arch between the fingers of Mercury and Apollo, traveling downward toward the line of heart. They are usually very short lines. On rare occasion, though, I have seen them connect to lines traveling through the line of life upwards, which indicates a squabble with relatives over money.

Some general marks affecting lines and formations

The following markings add additional meanings or provide clues to the overall reading of certain lines and markings. They either add or subtract strength and energy to a particular line or mount. Many are temporary; they disappear when they are no longer needed or when they become unimportant to the individual. (See Graphic #42.)

Breaks in the lines

Breaks in any lines (A) signify weaknesses at the time of they appear. Backup lines (B) and squares (L) serve as protection to breaks in the lines.

Chained formations

When chained formations (C), appear they disrupt the steady flow of the line. On the line of life, they represent health problems; on the line of heart, problems in relationships; with the line of head and fate, trouble with work or career for the time they appear.

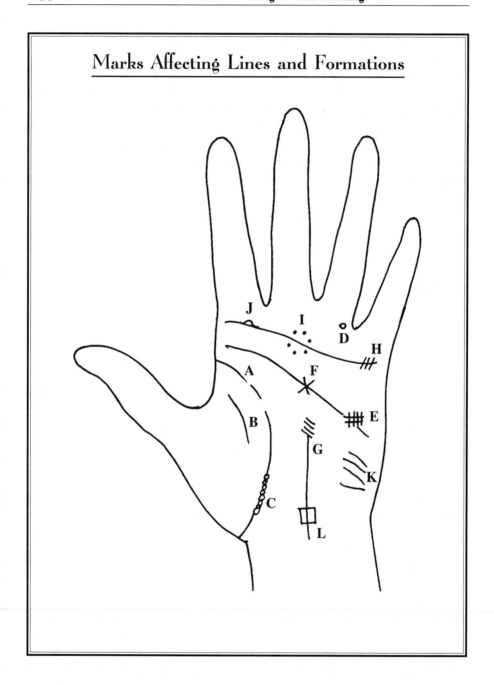

Graphic #42.

Marks affecting lines and formations.

Circles

In many cases, circles (D) maintain the same meaning as islands (J)—unless they appear on the mounts of the hands, in which case they are considered fortunate signs relating to the quality of that particular mount. For instance, on the mount of Apollo, circles add to a person's overall artistic capabilities. The opposite is true of solid circles, which sap energy. The effects of solid circles, though, can be temporary. Solid circles are tiny with no naturally colored skin showing through. They are darker than the skin tone. Regular circles are like islands on a line, only round.

Cross bars

Cross bars, grills, or grids (E) usually restrict the energy of a major line or mount. However, they can also be helpful marks when they appear on an excessively full mount of Jupiter or when the finger of Jupiter is extremely long. In those cases, leadership ability is held in check so that a person doesn't become overbearing with the excess energy already present. Cross bars on the mount of Luna add to the existing energy.

Crosses

Crosses (F) are temporary disturbances that can appear on lines, mounts, or other markings. More often than not, they fade away, sometimes within days. Crosses show a temporary setback or interference on the marking on which they appear. For instance, a cross on the mount of Luna might mean a short hiatus from creative thinking. A cross on the mount of Jupiter could mean a setback in the person's leadership. A cross on the line of life could mean a temporary illness.

Frayed lines

Frayed lines (G) appearing on major lines show loss of energy for the time they appear. They are not as strong as islands or breaks.

Ladders

Ladders (H) are similar to frayed lines in that they lessen energy at the time they appear, but they don't suggest permanency as islands or breaks do. Appearing randomly and either vertically, horizontally, or slanted, ladders indicate short disruptions for the areas in which they appear. If, for instance, a ladder appears on the line of fate, the person may be headed in a different direction than anticipated, such as a mother who planned to be a stay-at-home mom but had to return to work.

Spots

Spots (I) can appear as one dot or a series of little dots. On the line of life they mean a period of poor health; on the lines of head or heart spots signify depression or stress related to the character traits of the particular line (perhaps caused by a crumbling romance or depression over a job). Spots are usually very temporary, so they needn't cause undue concern.

Islands

Islands (J) are similar to chained formations in that they weaken the line at the time of their appearance. On the line of life, they indicate illnesses. They also show illnesses when they appear on the lines of heart or head, but illnesses related to the character of those lines. Appearing on the line of head, islands may denote problems with the career due to an illness; on the line of heart, they indicate trouble with a romantic relationship or a friendship.

Squares

Squares (L) are marks of preservation wherever they appear. If a square surrounds an island, circle, spot, or any other energy-sapping marking, it lessens the negative effect.

Travel lines

Travel lines are usually fairly short lines on the mount of Luna between the line of fate and the percussion side of the hand. They can also arise from the wrist bracelets. They remain faint lines unless the journey had a big impact on the person's life. Usually when they are present, it means travel to another country. All travel lines, however, don't show on people's hands who have made traveling a big part of their lives, whether the travel be for pleasure or work-related.

Numerous travel lines indicate that the person travels a great deal for business or pleasure. Other markings will determine which, such as a strong line of fate indicating success in business or a line heading toward Mercury that shows financial stability.

Travel lines that end in an island mean that the journey was not what was anticipated. When they end in a square, the person is protected from some type of danger, and when they end in a cross, the journey will be disappointing. (I've found that most of the trips that end in disappointment are connected to business. Fewer taken for pleasure end in disappointment.)

The most significant travel line I ever encountered was on the hand of a man from Europe whose line showed an enormous square at the end of the line, which itself was as deep and significant as any on the hand, including the line of life. The man had several other squares, which are marks of preservation, on other lines. I simply told him that around the age of 20 he was on a journey across water that nearly took his life. Because other markings indicated tragedy and unhappiness near that same time in his life (he was about 60 when I read his hand), I said that those same years were among the most unhappy and treacherous of his entire life.

As it turned out, when he was 19 and in the military (during World War II), he was captured by the Germans and transported by ship to a concentration camp. He'd just lost his best buddy, whose head was blown off right next to him, and the ship on which he was being transported was torpedoed. He was picked up in the water by the Allies and saved. The man eventually came to the United States following the war and became an insurance agent.

That's a bit dramatic for usual readings, but the memory has stayed with me.

CHAPTER 9

THE QUADRANTS, QUADRANGLE, AND GREAT TRIANGLE

The quadrangle and great triangle make up the center of the palm, with the quadrangle in the upper portion lying horizontally between the lines of head and heart, and the triangle at its widest, taking up the very center of the palm. The triangle is bordered by the lines of head and life.

The quadrants, another division of the hand, separate it into four meaningful categories. We look for a balance of lines and formations among the quadrants, so when one area appears more developed than another, it signifies an imbalance.

The quadrants

The four quadrants involve the upper and lower portions of the palm, plus the two sides. The lower portion of the palm deals with earthly matters, physical stamina, and the unconscious mind. The upper portion contends with the intellect, philosophy, spirituality, and the active, conscious mind.

For example, when the lines of heart and head, plus a portion of the line of life, lie in the upper part of the palm, they are tied to the intellect. If the majority of the line of head sits in the lower portion of the palm, though, the judgments are far more emotional, leaning toward earthly, practical matters and pushing the intellect aside.

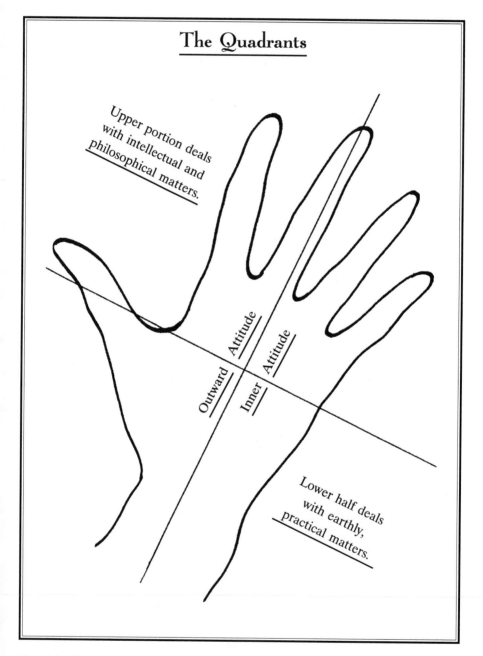

The Quadrants

Upper portion deals with intellectual and philosophical matters.

Outward Attitude

Inner Attitude

Lower half deals with earthly, practical matters.

Graphic #43. The quadrants.

The palm is separated into four categories, each with special meanings to the hand reader.

Another way of looking at it is that the upper portion is active (decision-making) and lower portion is receptive (letting things "just happen"). For instance, the major portion of the mount of Venus deals with passion and energy, which is very human and Earth-bound. The majority of it sits in the lower half of the palm. But the upper portion is still at work, trying to form rational decisions in cooperation with the more passionate, energetic side.

Both the upper and lower quadrants are necessary for our sojourn on Earth. It's important to use intellect and philosophic nature to make many decisions, but we also need to rely on our intuition and gut feelings sometimes. Still, it's not always in our best interest to be guided by our emotions. In retrospect, when we let emotions reign, we often wish we'd used our heads instead.

The other two quadrants define the outward and inward attitudes, and also the type of energy we use. The area for the outward attitude shares space with the mount of Venus, the thumb, the finger of Jupiter, and part of the finger of Saturn. These are all areas that deal with human relations. This side of the palm is the face we show to the public.

The other side of the hand, containing the mount of Luna, the little finger (Mercury), the ring finger (Apollo), and part of Saturn deals with the person's imagination, the artist within, and our personal thoughts. It represents the inner directed energy.

Putting the quadrants together

Sometimes a glance at a person's hand to determine the most active quadrant can reveal what direction the reading will take. A hand that appears more active by being fuller or more heavy with lines or other markings in one area than another pinpoints a person's priorities. Say the percussion side of the hand beneath the little finger running down to the wrist seems fuller and tauter than any other area of the hand. That person is inner-directed and imaginative. This is, after all, the area for the mount of Luna, which directs the imagination.

Perhaps the most active portion lies across from Luna in the lower portion of Venus. This might signify that the person, at least at the time of the reading, is more concerned with earthly, practical matters involving some very concrete decision-making. If most of the markings, including the major lines, are found in the lower quadrant, however, the person may be base in making judgments.

Inner/outer and Earthly/philosophic—that is, whether a person's inner or outer life is most meaningful to him or her and whether he is more Earth-based or philosophical—distinctions add to the store of knowledge that the hands show. These are important concepts to be dealt with, because the quadrants show what is driving the person at the time of the reading. Being aware of these distinctions can make the hand reading richer.

The quadrangle

The flat space between the head and heart lines on the palm comprises the quadrangle. The area is at its best when smooth, with few lines crossing it. An even disposition and intelligence are shown when it remains fairly even. The quadrangle also represents a nonjudgmental, broadminded, and accepting nature.

When the quadrangle narrows, so does the individual's view of the world; the narrower it gets, the more it leads to bigotry, judging others, and abruptness.

The quadrangle usually sits in the upper portion of the palm, standing for the person's intellectual and philosophical bent.

Palm readers typically deal with very few palms that show narrowed quadrangles, because the types of people who have them usually aren't open enough to get their palms read.

Through more than 30 years of palm reading, I've had the pleasure of reading the hands of bricklayers, attorneys, waitresses, superior court judges, politicians, engineers, housewives, writers, artists, professors, weavers, electricians, contractors, and just about every profession imaginable. Politically, they've been a mixed bag, and no particular persuasion holds a concession on being nonjudgmental, broad-minded, and accepting of others.

The great triangle

The great triangle, also referred to as the "plain of Mars," encompasses what is usually the thinnest portion of the hand in the center of the palm measured from the palm side to the back of the hand. The triangle lies between the line of life and line of head. Its narrowest point is beneath the finger of Jupiter, with the widest part opening toward the mount of Luna.

In palmistry lore, in the same approximate area as the great triangle, but with the addition of the line of heart, the top points of the letter "M"

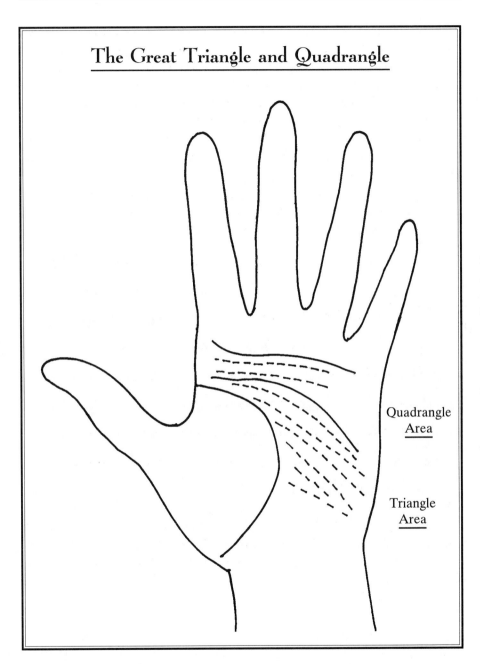

The Great Triangle and Quadrangle

Quadrangle
Area

Triangle
Area

Graphic #44. The great triangle and quadrangle.

The great triangle and the quadrangle provide clues about how people view the world and their niche in it.

are formed by the line of head, the line of heart, and the upper portion of the line of life in a few hands. It has been thought to be a sign of excellence and success. However, I've never found it to be that telling of a person's success in life. Too many other formations and lines intertwine to determine whether or not a person is successful, and then a definition of what constitutes success would be necessary.

However, a well-balanced, smoothly tapering triangle is the sign of intelligence, good health, and a certain amount of luck, especially if the lines forming it are clear and deep.

Within this great triangle lies another story, a Chinese tale that I've heard told in several different ways, chiefly relating to people who are extremely sensitive to their surroundings and to other people.

A tai chi master once trapped a small bird in the hollow of his hand. The hollow was extremely thin, especially in comparison to the well-developed mounts surrounding it. But the hollow was so thin that the master could also feel the bird's feet on the other side of his hand.

The story has also been told that the master's tai chi moves were so subtle and sensitive that every time the bird tried to fly away by pressing against the hand, the master lowered the triangle just enough to prevent the bird from being able to fly away. Finding no resistance to launch itself, the bird stayed in the palm of the master's hand.

I have seen people with this very thin hollow in the center of the hand; they're usually philosophers or deeply spiritual people. Former King Hussein of Jordan appeared from photos to have this thin hollow in the center of his palm.

CHAPTER 10

THE RIGHT FIT AT WORK

*Twenty years from now you will be more disappointed by the
things that you didn't do than by the ones you did do.
So throw off the bowlines. Sail away from the safe harbor.
Catch the trade winds in your sails. Explore. Dream. Discover.*

—Mark Twain

Studying hands breaks down stereotypes. We can be fooled when we think that people involved in specific kinds of work will have certain types of hands. Humans are much more complicated than that.

Federal Reserve Chairman Alan Greenspan's (one of biggest players in the U.S. economy) hands provided me with proof of how even someone adept at reading hands can be fooled by preconceived ideas. He's a brilliant man heeded by presidents, politicians, businesspeople, economists, investors, and most of the general public. When he speaks, the world listens.

If you'd assume Alan Greenspan has long fingers and thumbs on a graceful Air/philosophic hand, forget it. His palms are Earth/square, full, and with short fingers and thumbs. The energy in his hands, shown by the extremely full mounts of Venus and Luna, is extraordinary. This is the mind at work, probably 24 hours a day. His fingertips are a mix of conic and square, indicating that he's hardworking and has an appreciation for beauty and the arts. The man's logical inclinations are shown by the length of the lower phalange on the thumb. The third phalange on the index finger, being the longest of the three, indicates a bent for economics, sometimes including commercialization. He's also an avid reader and a philosophic type, as shown by the thumb bump on the bottom joint of the thumb.

Presidential fodder

Once past the rhetoric of our current and former presidents and presidential candidates, a look at their hands on television and in photos can reveal a great deal about their personalities and the type of leadership skills they might possess. Some of their idiosyncrasies might not seem to fit our preconceived notions of them, but they do share some commonalities.

President George W. Bush

Bush's hands appear to be Earth/square, with mostly square fingertips, which makes him a hard worker who has a love of the outdoors. Because the squareness is so pronounced, he can be a hard taskmaster. Although he might not be full of innovative ideas, he works well with others (as shown by the small space, or arch, between his little finger and ring finger) and will make decisions through consensus, although those he listens to must be somewhat like-minded for him to feel comfortable with their opinions.

The well-developed joints on Bush's fingers indicate attention to detail and an inquisitive mind. The most prominent knuckle sits below the index finger, showing a person who has strong convictions and is dependable.

Bush's thumb, like his father's, is stiff-jointed, indicating that he doesn't make close friends easily, but that when he does, he is loyal to them and keeps them for life. The thumb also indicates a bit of stubbornness, and once his mind is made up, it's not easy to dissuade him.

His little finger is quite long, making it easy for him to speak in public. He's a natural storyteller and loves to hear good stories from others, as well as a few good jokes.

Al Gore, former vice president

Gore's palms are full and thick, Air/philosophic, with raised pads on nearly all of the mounts, showing a love of beauty and the arts as well as a variety of interests. He's more concerned with the big picture and is not so concerned with minute details, which he leaves up to others.

He's tactful, as shown by the pads on the inside tips of his fingers, which are a mixture of square and conic. If crossed, though, he could display quite a temper. The thumb bump in the lower portion of the thumb indicates someone who is well read and who can see and understand various points of view, even though he will form his own opinions. In fact, sometimes he's overly opinionated, as shown by the length of the index finger. However, that same finger also indicates strong leadership abilities.

The mount of Luna, opposite the thumb on the percussion side of Gore's hand, is well developed, providing a good imagination. He is, however, more conservative than one might suspect, as shown by the tightness in the arch between the thumb and index finger.

Bill Clinton, former president

Clinton's elongated palm is a full and fairly thick Air/philosophic with well-developed mounts. His fingertips are mostly square, making him an indefatigable worker, always full of ideas and innovations. His index finger is exceptionally long and conic, making him a natural leader who enjoys the spotlight. The wide space in the arch between the little finger and ring finger indicates extreme independence; he is not a team player. His thumb is large, well formed, and bends backward easily, meaning that he makes friends easily, but, because of his independence, he is not an easy person to work with. The thumb's large size also shows great mental acuity and reasoning.

Clinton's fingers are smooth-jointed, meaning that he's adept at sizing up the big picture, but will leave details to others.

The well-developed mount of Venus at the bottom of the thumb on the palm side shows a passion for life. It is accompanied by a well-padded mount of Luna, opposite Venus on the little finger side of the palm, indicating a vivid imagination and a tendency to daydream.

George H. Bush, former president

Bush's palms are Water/conic, with mostly conic-tipped fingers, indicating an appreciation of the arts. The small-raised mount beneath the ring finger, which is considered the artistic finger, also indicates an artistic bent. Because the hands and fingers are extremely padded, he enjoys more than a little luxury. This is a man who speaks easily in front of others, as shown by the long little finger, but who really doesn't like to exert his authority, evidenced by his index finger, which is not overly long, as it is on the hands of many leaders. It is square-tipped, however, making him hardworking on the tasks at hand.

His thumb is straight, with no arch at the joint, meaning that he doesn't make friends easily. However, the ones he does make are lifetime friends, and he is loyal to them through thick and thin. He's a team player, because the little finger is balanced in space between it and the ring finger.

The puffiness displayed in the lower portions of his fingers (closest to the palms) indicates allergies to certain foods that he ingests.

His line of life, curving around the thumb, shows abundant energy and good health, although he works best in spurts of energy interspersed by long periods of rest.

Jimmy Carter, former president

Carter's hands are Air/philosophic, full, and well padded, indicating a very active mind. The thumb is straight, indicating that, as with the senior Bush, he is loyal to friends. He has an easier time making friends, because the space between the thumb and index finger is not as tight as Bush's. The tip of his thumb flattens out, which means that he has a difficult time finishing tasks that he begins. Because his mind is so active, he often starts too many projects and becomes overly involved in a multitude of them.

A shorter-than-usual little finger (it doesn't reach the first joint of the ring finger) shows that he is more shy than most people who enter politics.

The inside tips of his fingers contain extra small pads, referred to as sensitivity pads, which indicate that he will go out of his way to avoid hurting someone's feelings.

Carter is probably the most open of all the former and sitting presidents, because his fingers, when the hands are raised in greeting, are straight, or even bend back a bit. Those of the others tend to curl slightly toward the palms with more of a "me" attitude.

A surprise to me is the long length of his fingernails, indicating a few indulgences, because I never envisioned Carter as a self-indulgent man.

Certain character traits can be found in the hands of all politicians

Having worked as a reporter covering elections from city councils to U.S. congressmen, I've discovered that the majority of them share a few commonalities. Most have long index fingers, indicating leadership ability. A majority have long little fingers (former President Carter is one of the exceptions), which provides them with natural public speaking abilities. A majority have fingers that curl in slightly (again, Carter is an exception) showing that they like the spotlight. Whatever type of palm they have, at least a few square fingertips are present, an indication of their hardworking natures.

Politicians share these qualities with a few other professions, such as ministers and religious leaders; actors and other celebrity types; non-fiction authors who go on the lecture circuit, such as business and self-improvement gurus (fiction writers mostly want to stay home and write); and hucksters, who have been with us forever selling snake oil and the like. The latter doesn't imply that I'm lumping hucksters with self-improvement gurus or ministers. It's just that they share some commonalities, such as the natural ability to speak before others, to persuade, to entertain, and to employ a shtick effectively.

Limelighters

We're not all presidential material, or hucksters, but we might share some of their same characteristics if we like the limelight. Also, people who enjoy being in charge of things, which entails certain leadership abilities (such as decision-making), are brethren of the limelighters. Not all can be bosses or prefer jobs involving speaking before large groups of people, but the following are some of the characteristics that make it easier.

▶ Long little fingers that extend slightly above the first joint of the ring finger. This provides the ability (and pleasure) of speaking in front of others.

▶ A long index finger (longer than the ring finger when the hand is in a relaxed position). This shows leadership abilities if it's tempered by a fairly flat mount beneath the finger or small lines forming a grill on the mount. If the finger is long and the mount quite large, the person might be overbearing as a boss.

▶ A wide arch between the index finger and the thumb. This shows an accepting, unbiased nature. If the thumb also arches backward easily, it means the individual is gregarious and makes friends easily. If the thumb is stiff, friendship comes harder, but the person might be more loyal and caring toward employees.

▶ An Earth/square palm or a few square fingertips on any type of palm help people with leadership abilities, because the square formation lends itself to hard work and plenty of energy, whether the task be mental or physical.

▶ A well-developed mount of Venus shows a strong life force and plenty of energy.

Independent workers

In 1831 Alexis de Tocqueville, author of *Democracy in America,* observed that Americans were impatient to get on with the task of settling the land and making it perform (and conform) to their visions. He also saw Americans as an independent lot. We're still trying to learn to work together.

Some people, however, are more independent than others, and they work better in their own businesses or enterprises. They tend not to be team players, even though they may like dealing with the public. It isn't that they prefer isolation so much, but that they enjoy making their own decisions and working their own hours, which usually amounts to far more than an eight-hour day. Also, they often possess an inordinate amount of energy and curiosity and quickly become bored in a routine job.

Self-employment can also include personalities that are not afraid of mixing with a variety of different type people. They need to be skilled networkers, however, because they don't have the advantage of a bustling office to stimulate ideas.

Self-employment carries more uncertainties than working for someone else, so high self-esteem is a plus.

Some of the hand characteristics for people who want to run their own businesses, be a consultant, or work from home include:

▶ A little finger with a wide arch between it and the finger of Apollo (ring finger). This shows independence.

▶ An index finger that is far longer than Apollo or that reaches beyond the first phalange on the finger of Saturn next to it. This indicates leadership abilities.

▶ A Fire/spatulate palm, especially when the widest portion is at the bottom of the hand, indicating people with vast supplies of creative ideas who would rather do it "their" way.

▶ A line of head moderately separated from the line of life at its beginning beneath the finger of Jupiter. This shows a characteristic of the risk-taker. If the space is too wide, however, the person doesn't plan enough and might have a tougher time making it as an independent.

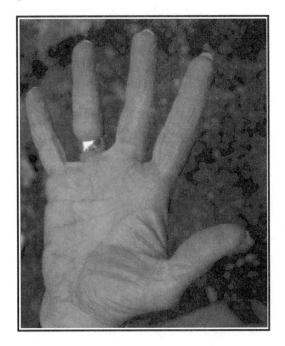

Graphic #45.

This is the hand of a former college counselor who decided to pursue her own catering and cheesecake business. She's been very successful. She's also politically involved, having served as a school trustee and a campaign coordinator for several politicians. The qualities in this woman's hand that add to her independence include a line of head that is separated from line of life beneath the finger of Jupiter at its start. The moderate separation makes her a risk-taker, but with risks that are of an intellectual and personal nature rather than a physical one, which would be shown with a far wider space. The fingers of Jupiter and Apollo are well balanced, indicating leadership ability without needing to have her own way all the time. She also knows how to delegate; she trusts the advice of others, as shown by the wide space between her thumb and index finger. This wide space, or arch, indicates a nonjudgmental nature and an acceptance of different types of people and ideas. The little finger is quite long, providing her with natural public speaking abilities.

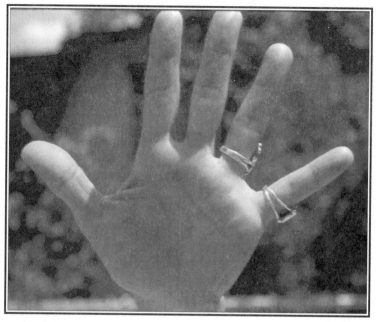

Graphic #46.

This is the hand of an extremely independent person, both in thought and spirit. She's an artist, writer, public speaker, and spiritual visionary. The little finger widely separated from the ring finger is a sure indication of an independent nature. Independence is even more pronounced when the person wears a ring on the little finger. (This is because rings worn on specific fingers can take on the meanings of those fingers and their particular placements and shapes. Likewise, if a ring is customarily worn on the index finger, it adds leadership capabilities and a belief in self.) The line of head is only slightly separated from the line of life beneath the finger of Jupiter. Her index finger is longer than the ring finger, giving her a strong belief in self. With this excessively long index finger, the separated lines of life and head, and the wide space between the little finger and that of Apollo, it would be very difficult for this person to work for someone other than herself. It's a very strong, capable hand. Something of note to check is the Old Soul mount running beneath the wrist on the percussion side of the hand (see Chapter 7). It's more rare than usual to discover this mount on anyone's hand.

A little more security, please

Some people work better for others or in an office setting. A friend, a computer analyst who troubleshoots for large companies throughout the world for a California firm, tried consulting on her own and decided she didn't like it. She had problems scheduling her time, allowed other activities to get in the way, had problems billing acquaintances, and missed the steady paycheck.

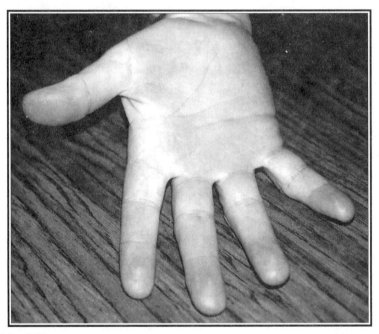

Graphic #47.

Another man, a loan executive, tried working from home, because he lived a great distance from the head office. He quickly became bored and distracted and missed the interplay of working with others. So he went back to commuting. Note that his lines of head and life are joined, indicating that he's more reserved and wants more security than the person whose lines of life and head are separated. His fingertips are square, showing that he's a diligent worker, and the tips also contain tactful pads, which means he doesn't like to hurt anyone's feelings. The line of head travels straight across the palm, providing a balanced disposition, a good sign for someone who deals in banking or loans. The little finger is separated from Apollo, which, even though he's not a risk-taker, shows that he's very independent in his personal life and dealings.

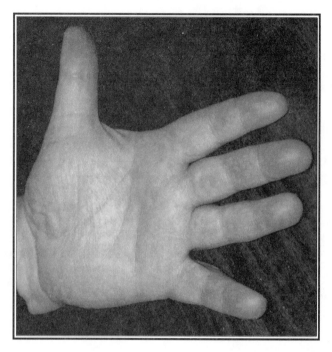

Graphic #48.

This hand belongs to a pilot who now flies for pleasure but who was a helicopter pilot in Vietnam, Alaska, and a variety of points around the globe. He's worked in the Arctic helicoptering scientists into strategic places and staying with them for months at a time until the weather warms enough to get out. He has also worked dousing forest fires, among other high-risk jobs.

However, his lines of life and head aren't separated as one might expect on the hands of a risk-taker. In reality, though, pilots are notorious for their careful planning. They check, double-check, and triple-check everything. No stone is left unturned, because they know it could mean their lives.

Also to note on the pilot's hand is the wide space between the little finger and the ring finger, which indicates independence. The thumb is straight, meaning that he doesn't make close friends easily but that he is loyal to the ones he does have. His fingertips are square and conic, making him hardworking and also artistic. Notice the slight curve of the line of head down toward the mount of Luna, which portends a good imagination. He's also a writer.

Touching base with your personal skills

We all have certain needs when it comes to our work, and we also have skills and personal attributes that we bring to the workplace that make us successful. A trait that might be good for one job could be a distraction for another. Or a trait that seems negative to some people might be necessary for certain jobs.

One of the biggest attributes anyone can have, according to career consultants, is "people skills." A professor of business economics told me that rather than parents encouraging their kids to prepare early for successful careers, they ought to encourage them to develop good people skills.

So when reading people's hands, we look for more than just an ability at math, or writing, or creativity, or the potential to fill a leadership role. To be really successful, people need other qualities to complement those basic skills. Much of the time, people aren't even aware of their non-academic abilities, or the life skills they have inadvertently accumulated. They way individuals view themselves may be far different from what is going to show in the hand.

Too often, we believe we're too old to make changes, too young to try something that seems to take many years of experience, or not smart enough, attractive enough, or pushy enough to become involved in certain types of work that really strike our fancy. Ask people about their weaknesses, though, and they are ready with a list of them.

Many people make successful career changes later in life. This fact validates the idea that we are more than we think we are. The hand can show the enormous talent, creativity, and other attributes, often before individuals are aware of them.

Professions and potential markings

Certain markings on the hands might be found in particular professions, especially when people are successful at that job. For instance, reporters, detectives, or research analysts might get a boost if their hands contain a line of curiosity, which is a short horizontal line found on the mount of Jupiter near the side of the hand (see Graphic #40 in Chapter 8). There are also a few other markings that might contribute to a person's curiosity, or make him or her particularly adept in a field that requires it, such as developed knuckles with the phalanges above and below them waist-shaped—in other words, the knuckles appear knobby-looking rather than smooth because the phalanges are much thinner.

We all have hand characteristics that make us above average in specific areas. They offer us an advantage if we're able to go into a type of work that fits our capabilities, needs, strengths, and personal proclivities. Not all people find the right fit; this is why some of us get stuck in jobs that drive us nuts. Circumstances, too, sometimes prevent us from "getting out." Also, for some professions a great deal of education is necessary, and the hand might show that certain people are going to struggle academically—not necessarily because they are any less smart than the next guy, but maybe because they don't have the patience and discipline required. Maybe their heart rules their head and they get married and begin a family before they are able to complete the education. Perhaps in later years, after the kids are grown, they return to school. This all might show on the hand. (See Chapter 6 about the line of fate.)

The following are only a few of today's professions. Obviously space limitations in this book preclude listing all of the thousands of professions available to individuals, but those selected offer characteristics of other types of work.

Accountant/investor/financial advisor

The individual's hand might contain a line of head that runs fairly straight across the hand or that curves up toward the finger of Mercury, indicating interest and ability with math and commerce. The fingers of Jupiter and Apollo might be fairly even in length, showing good balance with money.

A physicist, chemistry teacher, or computer programmer could also show the straight or curving upward line of head but not necessarily the balance with money.

Anthropologist/archaeologist

An anthropologist or archaeologist requires an inordinate amount of patience, because it often takes several years before findings can be confirmed. Although there are many types of anthropologists (some who do most of their work in offices; others work in the field), we generally think of them out in the wilds taking part in a dig. If so, we're probably seeing not only a patient person, but someone who also likes a certain amount of adventure, which could be shown by separated lines of head and life.

Architect

Architects have their heads in more than one world, those of the mathematician and the artist. So although they're going to be disciplined with mathematical abilities (and more often than not to have a straight line of head), the line may slope slightly or send branches toward the mount of Luna for imagination. If the line of head slopes, it's likely that a branch heads toward Mercury. Renowned architects such as Frank Lloyd Wright or R.M. Schindler could also have a wide space between the little finger and ring finger, showing independence, and maybe a good length to the first phalange of the thumb, because they seemed to have shared a bit of stubbornness, according to their biographies and other accounts of their work and personalities.

Attorney

Despite a few jokes rumbling around the country and the Internet today, attorneys don't have crooked little fingers (which indicate a liar) to any more degree than the rest of the population. Most are hardworking, probably with a few square-tipped fingers. Trial lawyers more than likely possess long little fingers, because they provide the gift of oratory. The majority of attorneys, though, never see a courtroom. Most of their work involves research and advice to large corporations or government officials. But for those who have a more public appearance, the long little finger (for public speaking), an Earth/square palm (tireless worker), and a long finger of Jupiter (leadership ability) are apparent.

Coach/athlete/chiropractor

Because most team coaches come from an athletic background, they tend to have larger hands and well-developed thumbs, which allow them greater control over basketballs, baseballs, footballs, and the like. But they aren't the only ones with those special hands. Many chiropractors and even a reflexologist I met one time had those large, malleable hands.

Other types of sports don't necessarily require large, malleable hands. Tennis great Bjorn Borg's palms are Air/philosophic with a mixture of square and conic fingertips. His thumb is not particularly large, and neither are the mounts on his hand.

Engineer/magician

For years engineers have been thought to be among the more conservative members of the population, politically and in their personal lives.

From the hands I've read, that mostly holds true. But in order to illustrate that likenesses exist where we might not expect them, consider that a majority of magicians tend to also be conservative and male. On the other hand, magicians generally have longer fingers than most, with square tips, and thumbs that are quite supple, not necessarily a trademark of engineers. Performing magicians like the limelight, so check out the section on limelighters earlier in this chapter for other proclivities in the hands.

Historian/investigative reporter/law-enforcement official

Historians are researchers, so many have developed joints and waist-like phalanges on the fingers. They want to dig into the truth of a matter and leave no stone unturned. They share this trait with investigative reporters and some law-enforcement officials who dig for facts and have good reasoning abilities. Some law-enforcement officials, such as FBI agents, might also have fairly straight lines of head, because many are accountants.

Interior designer

The lines of head for good interior designers naturally slope a little toward the mount of Luna, providing the imagination that can turn a dump into a dream. They're usually "people" people who enjoy dealing with the public and adept talkers, so they tend to have long little fingers and thumbs that bend back easily. Look for well-developed mounts and a few conic fingertips, because they need an artist's perspective.

Religious leader/politician/actor

Fundamentalist preachers usually have smaller arches between the index finger and thumb, as they tend to be a little more narrow-minded than, say, a minister from an Episcopalian church or a Catholic priest. A more liberal Jewish rabbi bears the large arch more so than his Orthodox counterpart. Most religious leaders, whether orthodox or more liberal, will have a long little finger, because speaking ability is a plus, a trait they share with politicians and actors, although the motives for speaking may be different.

Scientist

Not only does being a scientist require mathematical ability, as is necessary for a great many professions, such as architects and accountants, but it requires the ability to absorb great amounts of information and to reach logical conclusions. Scientist Theodore P. Stecher theorized in 1965 that graphite must be present in the interstellar medium and that it was absorbing light at that wavelength, making it a player in the development of stars. He had to wait a quarter of a century until the telescopes aboard the space shuttle *Columbia* confirmed his theory. So we're looking at people with straight lines of head, possibly with branches headed toward Luna, with the second phalange of the thumb longer than first, because this speaks of a logical mind and patience.

I noted the exceptionally long second thumb phalange on the hand of Rita Colwell, director of the National Science Foundation. Her palms are Earth/square, with mostly conic fingertips, and her little finger is widely separated from the ring finger. Plus the little finger is quite long. In all, those markings make her a hard worker with a love for the arts and an independent nature. Her thumb also carries the thumb bump, or philosopher's bump, making her an avid reader.

Sculptor/painter/weaver

A sculptor might need strong hands, as opposed to some other types of artists. Nearly all artists' hands I've read have sloping lines of head and a mixture of conic and square-tipped fingers. The palm can be Earth/square, Air/philosophic, or Fire/spatulate to supply the needed energy for the work that it takes to be an artist. Although artistic endeavors to those not involved might seem less demanding than other types of work (that's partly because most artists love their work), they actually involve demanding discipline and extreme amounts of energy. Sir Winston Churchill, who in his later years became noted for some of his paintings, said he had trouble getting started until a well-known artist told him to not be timid when he faced the blank canvas. He told him to "attack" the canvas.

This is only a sampling of some of the characteristics that might be found in the hands of people with certain types of jobs. But individuals are made up of more than their professions, so we need to look deeper when reading the hands.

CHAPTER 11

MARRIAGE AND LOVE

COMPATIBILITY

Some day, after we have mastered the winds,
the waves, the tides and gravity we shall
harness the energies of love. Then, for
the second time in history of the world,
man will have discovered fire.

—Teilhard de Chardin

What it takes to make love work

Opposites might attract, but statistically, they don't make the best marriages or loving associations. There are always exceptions to the rule, and all of us know couples with rich, lasting relationships who seem to have little in common, but they're not the norm. The majority of lasting associations includes like traits among the couple, according to marriage and family research. People who come from the same type of family backgrounds; hold the same religious beliefs (or none); enjoy the same types of recreation; have similar energy levels; and enjoy near educational levels to one another stand better chances at lasting associations.

Some of the things that once held couples together through thick and thin (such as certain divisions of labor, with the woman taking care of the home and the man responsible for supporting the family financially) no longer work. Part of this is due to changing economic opportunities for women, making it possible for them to leave strife-ridden or abusive marriages.

Cohabitation has become commonplace within the last 40 years in the United States. Currently, more than eight million unmarried male/female couples live together. That figure shows an increase of 72 percent between 1990 and 2000. The number of unmarried couples living together has increased 10-fold since 1960, according to the U.S. Census.

The same trends in the United States are reflected in other industrialized countries. *Population Trends* reports that 14 percent of all couple households in Britain cohabit, a figure that is expected to increase by 90 percent over the next 20 years.

Strong relationships require some of the following:

▶ Marriage after age 20.

▶ Education past high school.

▶ Established career or working goals.

▶ Contentment (that is, not looking for someone to make him or her happy).

▶ A stable marriage between the individual's parents.

▶ Close family ties.

▶ No excessive alcohol or illegal drug use.

▶ Similar religious affiliation/beliefs.

▶ Similar future goals and flexibility.

▶ Being sociable rather than a loner.

▶ Approval of the association by friends and family.

▶ Not overly impulsive, self-conscious, or anxious.

▶ Similar gender role attitudes and ideas.

▶ Interest in sex.

Many, but not all, of the characteristics in the preceding list will show directly on a person's hand, such as the energy level, as indicated by a firm mount of Venus or a deep and distinct line of life. On the other hand, it's difficult to tell much about the partner of the person's hand being read. For instance, the reader couldn't determine whether the couple shares the same religious affiliation.

The predispositions for lasting marriages or love associations are many, although not all of them can be found on one particular marking in the hand. Sometimes it's a compilation of characteristics that show the adaptability for compatibility, or the earlier life that may have shaped the individual's outlook on marriage and love associations.

Age of marriage

The age at which Americans marry has been steadily increasing, and the age difference between men and women has been narrowing. In 1950, the average age for women to marry was little more than 20 years old; it was nearly 23 for men. By 1998, the average age for women was 25, and it was nearly 27 for men.

The number of women living alone doubled between 1970 and 1998 from 7.3 million to 15.3 million. The number of women ages 45 to 64 living alone is expected to increase by 65 percent over the next 10 years, according to the 2000 census.

A look at the growth of singles and unmarried people shows that in 2000, 51.7 percent of the adult population tied the knot—down from 78.2 percent in 1950. The reverse exists for the growth in singles: 48.3 percent in 2000 compared to 21.8 percent in 1950.

To determine the approximate age of marriage on a person's hand, check the placement of the marriage lines that lie horizontally beneath the little finger (Mercury), and above the line of heart on the outside edge of the percussion side of the hand. Those that lie less than halfway between the bottom crease on the little finger and the line of the heart account for deep, lasting love prior to the age of 30. Those beneath the midpoint take place after the age of 30. (For reference to age lines as shown on relationship lines, see the Appendix. Also see Chapter 8.)

Again, only the deep lines account for lasting associations that impact the life.

Education past high school

An education past high school allows individuals more time for mature development and to find out who they really are, what they want from life, and what they are capable of. Continued education increases the chances of meeting more diverse people and making greater preparations for life.

More opportunities become available. This increases self-esteem, self-awareness, and self-assurance, all of which add to the chances of a successful marriage.

Some markings that indicate continued education are the fine lines arising from the line of life headed in the direction of the finger of Jupiter. If the continued education is prior to the age of 25 or so (or directly out of high school), the lines will appear at the beginning of the line of life, which means lifelong learning and education. (For ages see the Appendix.)

Established career or working goals

Established working goals are also important. Individuals who develop a life plan and are planning to take care of themselves, regardless of when and if they marry or establish a permanent bond, tend to have steadier relationships when they *do* choose to have them. Life plans, of course, can—and do—change, but making them from the onset shows stability, which is one of the attributes of couples who stay together.

A few markings that might indicate early planning include a line of fate that begins fairly close to the wrist, whether it stems from the middle of the palm or from the mount of Luna. Other lines of fate can spring from the initial one or from other places in the palm, which can show career changes, or directions, but the initial strong beginning shows stability.

Contentment with self

People who are happy with themselves, and free from wants, may still want to become part of a couple, but they are better prepared to make the right choices when they don't feel desperate to be with someone. This, of course, changes through the years. An older person who has previously been married and either widowed or divorced may not plan (or even want) to be married again. Although a growing number of people, especially women, are choosing to never marry, or not to remarry, a majority of never-married women do plan, at some point in their lives, to marry and have children.

Stable marriage between parents

Research clearly shows that an individual's chance of a stable marriage is enhanced if he or she came from an intact and happy family. It's not guaranteed, of course, and some families that appear happy on the surface are tumultuous inside the home, but on the whole, it does increase the likelihood of a lasting marriage or partnership.

An indication of a troubled childhood or erratic family life can show itself in the middle of the palm near the wrist by several small, but distinct lines coming together and crisscrossing one another. Also, little hairlines drooping from the line of the heart can sometimes indicate problems of trust caused by troubled childhoods, sometimes, but not always, based on problems in the parental home. These drooping hairlines, however, can also be caused by learning to mistrust love interested due to previous betrayals. This is especially true of people with poor self-esteem or neurotic personalities.

Close family ties

Close family ties that are not excessively demanding or neurotic (as identified as anxiety, depression, impulsiveness, stress, and anger/hostility) result in stability and appreciation for others, according to studies conducted at Brigham Young University. Close family ties also promote adaptability, acceptance, and warmth, all of which are strong attributes for healthy associations. Those ties are mostly shown by the closeness or separateness of the line of fate as it runs up the palm parallel to the line of life. This only applies to about the midway point on the palm, because from there on it heads away from the line of life. When the line of fate is extremely close, and running parallel, to the line of life, it might show some family interference, because the adult child leans too much on the parent(s). The opposite would be when the space is excessively wide between the two lines, which stands for alienation from the parent(s). Often, the space between the two will change, being close in the younger years and then jutting away from the line of life, showing separation, much later. Also, the lines can show a separation at some point and then a joining, as if at some point in the person's life, usually when he or she is older, of making contact and becoming close with the parents once again. (See Graphic #35 in Chapter 6.)

No excessive alcohol or drug use

It goes without saying that dysfunctional families are frequently the result of addictions such as alcohol and/or illegal drug use. But other addictions, too, get in the way of healthy mating, such as gambling, which is gaining notoriety in the U.S. medical and psychological communities as one of the fastest-growing addictions. A propensity for alcohol or drug addiction is frequently shown by a sharp angle on the hand adjacent to the wrist beneath the thumb. An extra long ring finger (Apollo), longer than the index finger, indicates a love of gambling.

Similar religious beliefs

Although more people in the Western world are accepting of other religious beliefs today, stability in a marriage or a love association is enhanced by commonalities. It may be difficult for, say, a Unitarian to see eye-to-eye with a born-again Fundamentalist, and vice versa. Although raging hormones may blur distinctions at first, research shows that for the majority of people, different religious beliefs can create problems later on, unless those involved share a great deal of tolerance for the other person's beliefs. This is best shown by a wide arch between the index finger and the thumb.

Similar future goals and flexibility

Although situations can change once a couple establishes themselves, those who discuss future plans and goals, such as whether or not (or when) to have children, how the work situation will be handled, where they want to live, and any number of preliminaries, begin the association with a head start, according to career studies. Ironically, studies also show that when family is selected in favor of money and career in importance—as young as high school—careers move ahead faster and the individuals end up making more money. Part of the reason is because a bad marriage can wreak havoc on a career.

The hands in Graphics #49 and 50 are representative of a couple, both with careers, who have four young sons and who planned how they would handle careers and a family long before they married, because they knew they wanted both. They even agreed how they would handle job moves. When the wife had an offer to accept a better position, he agreed to the move. Later, when he was offered a prime position, they moved across country to his job's location.

Being sociable rather then a loner

Finding out if a person is sociable, rather than a loner, can be determined by several markings. (See Chapter 10 for more information.) People with wide arches between the thumb and index finger, plus a thumb that bends backward easily into an arch, are the most social of all. People with straight, unbending thumbs can also be sociable, but not to the same degree. The arch between the thumb and index finger is very telling, because when it is tight, the person can be judgmental of others. Tactful pads, those extra little pads on the inside of fingertips that make individuals

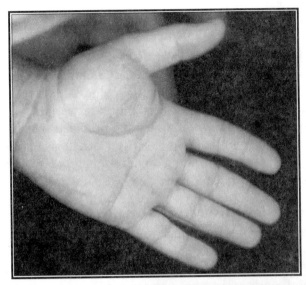

**Graphic #49.
Husband.**

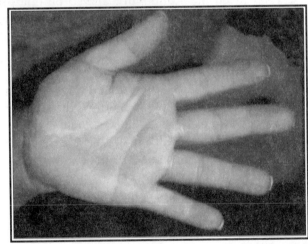

**Graphic #50.
Wife.**

Graphics #49 and 50. *The likenesses in this couple's hands (although there are also some differences) include similar thumbs that show flexibility in the arch between the thumb and index finger; fingers of Apollo and Jupiter that are about the same length, showing balance in finances and leadership; well-developed mounts, especially Venus and Luna, indicating lots of energy and imagination; and lines of heart that aren't demanding of the other person, because they don't run into the finger of Jupiter. The major difference in their hands is that the lines of life and head are separated in hers, making her more of a risk-taker than her husband, whose lines are joined beneath the finger of Jupiter.*

who have them more diplomatic and sensitive to others, can also be a plus for a sociable person. A long little finger that goes to or beyond the first phalange of the ring finger can also be a good sign, as it makes it easy for them to speak in front of others.

The feel of a palm, whether it is warm to the touch or cold, hard or soft, pink-tinged or white, can also indicate sociability. For warmth in a person, look for a warm palm (weather permitting and provided that the person has no circulation problems) that is pinkish and that feels elastic to the touch. Keep in mind, however, that Air/philosophic and Water/conic hands will be spongier than Earth/square or Fire/spatulate hands.

Not overly impulsive, self-conscious, or anxious

Impulsiveness can be shown in a very wide space between the lines of head and life when those lines are separated. A moderate or small space, however, doesn't mean impulsiveness. Rather, it shows a propensity to take risks in business and work and to be open to new ventures. Self-consciousness can be shown by an extremely short little finger. Numerous small lines spread all over the palm show anxiety.

Similar gender role attitudes and ideas

Sexist attitudes and old-fashioned roles for men or women are becoming obsolete in most of the Western world, where more women than ever before are working and where Dad sometimes serves as the chief caretaker for the kids. This doesn't mean that a woman can't be a stay-at-home mom and still enjoy the changed status of women—or that a man can't be a hospital nurse and still be as masculine as a male prizefighter. It means that we have choices. Also, these same attitudes of choice and openness also affect same-sex couples. The major thing to look for in the hand of any partner would be a good arch between the thumb and index finger, as that shows acceptance and not being judgmental of others. A healthy attitude toward a partner could also include a strong line of heart that doesn't end beneath the finger of Apollo or thereabouts. An extremely short line of heart indicates coldness in matters of the heart. When the line of the heart is quite long, though, extending to the beneath the finger of Jupiter, it means that the person has extremely high ideals in a partner and, depending on other lines, could be very demanding. Also, lines of heart with chained formations, breaks, or a multitude or hairlines drooping from the line indicate problems of trust.

Interest in sex

Obviously a good sex life plays an important part in most long-term love associations. But what some term "good" varies among people. Without going into the nuances of how much, how long, what kind, etc. the following questionnaire will help you understand your own sexual interest, according to palm reading. Pick only the choice that best fits the description of what is on your hand.

Examine the shapes of your fingers. Yours are:
    a. Puffy at the base.
    b. Puffy at the base and inside tip.
    c. Flat at the base.
    d. Flat at the base, yet puffy at the tip.

Your thumb is:
    a. Straight and not flexible, but has a wide arch between the thumb and index finger.
    b. The arch is narrow, but the thumb itself is flexible and bends backward at the joint.
    c. Straight and not flexible, with a narrow arch between it and the index finger.
    d. Flexible, with a wide arch between it and the index finger.

The mount of Venus beneath your thumb is:
    a. Hard and flat.
    b. Firm, yet elastic.
    c. Full and springy.
    d. Very fleshy feeling.

The color of your palm is:
    a. Pale in color.
    b. Yellowish.
    c. Pinkish.
    d. Red.

The girdle of Venus (see Graphic #40 in Chapter 8) is:
    a. Clearly marked and quite deep.
    b. Faint and stunted.
    c. Broken into more than one line.
    d. Not present at all.

Your line of heart is:

    a.   Well delineated and pinkish in color.

    b.   Heavier and deeper than the line of head.

    c.   Faint in depth and color.

    d.   Chained or has little hairlines drooping from it.

Your line of heart:

    a.   Terminates in a fork beneath the finger of Saturn or the finger of Jupiter.

    b.   Terminates beneath the finger of Apollo.

    c.   Heads straight for the finger of Jupiter.

    d.   Proceeds nearly straight across the palm, stopping on the far side of Jupiter.

Your line of life:

    a.   Swings out nearly to the middle of the palm.

    b.   Hugs fairly close to the thumb.

    c.   Is unbroken as it travels down the palm.

    d.   Contains some breaks or islands.

The mount of Luna opposite Venus is:

    a.   Full and spongy.

    b.   Flatter than Venus.

    c.   Pink-tinged.

    d.   Padded nearly to beneath the finger of Mercury.

Your line of head:

    a.   Is separated from the line of life.

    b.   Is attached to the line of life.

    c.   Runs into the line of life into the mount of Luna.

    d.   Is far more delineated than the line of heart.

Your line or lines for love associations (see Graphic #41 in Chapter 8):

    a.   Are few, strong, and deep.

    b.   Are more than five.

    c.   Contain drooping hairlines.

    d.   Are short.

Your palm contains:

- a. Many horizontal lines on the mount of Luna.
- b. Many horizontal lines on the percussion side of the hand beneath the line of heart.
- c. Horizontal lines on the mount of Luna and the percussion side of the hand.
- d. None of the above.

Scoring

Give yourself points as follows:

1. a-3, b-4, c-1, d-2
2. a-3, b-3, c-1, d-4
3. a-1, b-4, c-4, d-2
4. a-2, b-1, c-4, d-2
5. a-4, b-2, c-3, d-1
6. a-4, b-2, c-2, d-1
7. a-4, b-1, c-2, d-3
8. a-4, b-1, c-3, d-2
9. a-3, b-2, c-3, d-4
10. a-4, b-3, c-1, d-2
11. a-4, b-4, c-3, d-2
12. a-3, b-3, c-1, d-2

31–48 points: Your temperament is to enjoy a good sex life, partly based on your own good self-esteem and libido. You tend not to be inhibited, and you look for partners with the same attitude.

20–30 points: Although you're mostly uninhibited and enjoy a good sex life, sometimes you're just too wrapped up in other things or tired to enjoy sex.

Less than 19: You might be too involved with other activities or have too much concern with a career, past hang-ups (even stemming from childhood), or perceived poor health to enjoy sex.

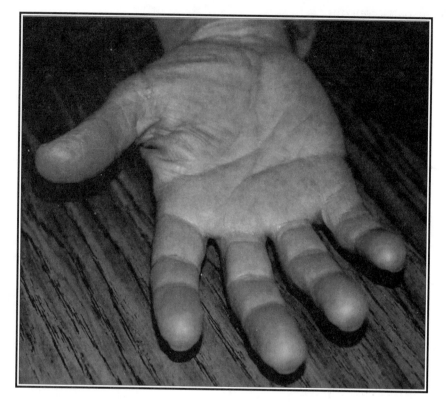

Graphics #51. Husband.

Graphics #51 and 52. *These are the hands of a couple who has enjoyed a thriving marriage for more than 40 years. Particularly take note of the lines of heart, both of which have fainter branches heading toward the index finger, but not running into it, indicating idealism in marriage, but not overly so, because the branch heading toward the index finger doesn't run into it, which would indicate an overabundance of idealism and expectations from the partner. The thumbs are shaped similar to one another, showing thumb bumps, which indicate an avid reader. They are, indeed, avid readers.*

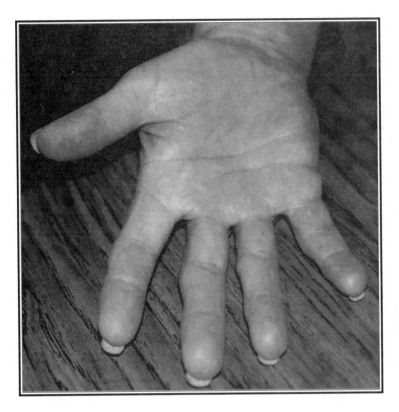

Graphics #52. Wife.

Also, both hands are Earth/square, making this couple hard workers. Even the percussion sides of their hands are shaped similarly, with the extra fullness of puff beneath the little finger, indicating a sense of humor.

The preceding graphics are examples of a couple who have many things in common, but it doesn't mean that all the same markings need be seen in a couple's hands for them to be compatible. Many different markings, as mentioned in this chapter, can indicate compatibility.

CHAPTER 12

ARMONIZING WITH FRIENDS

Friendship improves happiness,
and abates misery,
by doubling our joys,
and dividing our grief.

— Joseph Addison

More often than not, close friends share a great deal in common with us, whether that involves socio/economic factors, ethics, type of work, leisure activities, children, education, and other likes and dislikes.

It's also more usual for friends to be of the same political persuasion (just as it's more common for husbands and wives to belong to *different* political parties). All one need do is look at national statistics on who votes for whom to see that women vote predominantly Democrat and more men vote Republican. This doesn't mean that many women aren't Republican, or that many couples don't share the same politics.

There are, though, a great many marriages or love partnerships where couples are the best of friends, which may be the ideal, but such relationships usually take on different characteristics than friendships between same sex genders. Outside of marriage or deep relationships, many men and women do carry on close friendships with the opposite sex, but it's not the norm, especially for married folks.

Friendship

Great friendships develop over time and are laced with equality. We're able to talk with friends on any level, because they listen with open hearts and minds. With friends, people can reveal deep feelings, good and bad, and they won't be castigated. Friends, though, won't take advantage by dumping too much, too soon, too often on one another.

Deep, lasting friendships don't form as readily when they are initiated by need, such as attendance at support groups. Those initial friendships may be very intense, but as the needs are served and some drift away from relying on the same level of support, the friendship often fades.

Friendships come in all shapes and sizes and are borne of many different circumstances. A few ingredients that allow friendships to flourish include, but are not limited to, the following:

▶ Grow over time.

▶ Are laced with equality.

▶ Make it possible for both to talk and share equally.

▶ Show empathy and tolerance toward each other.

▶ Make it possible to listen with eyes, ears, and emotions.

▶ Are there for us, but not if we demand too much.

▶ Enable us to reveal feelings, but only when enough time has been spent developing the friendship.

▶ Stay together in spirit, even when they are apart.

▶ Help to keep our lives going.

▶ Allow us to speak to one another without talking.

▶ Build trust in one another over time.

▶ Are nonjudgmental of the friend.

▶ Can argue and still remain friends.

What characteristics make people good friends?

The following are only a few of the qualities people look for within friendships, and they are characteristics that can be found in the hand. Not any one person is going to have all of them, nor are all the markings going to be found on any one hand. Friendship involves accepting a person's faults, too, of which all of us have many. But at some point in a developing friendship, certain characteristics, beliefs, personality traits, interests, and idiosyncrasies blend with those of another, and a friendship is born.

Sharing similar values

Determining what constitutes values can be a mixed bag. Religiosity can be an important value for some; diversity in spiritual beliefs, or no particular belief system, could be a value to others. Acceptance of a person's sexual orientation could be a value for one person, but not to another. Values, then, are much like ethics and integrity: One person's ethics or definition of integrity might be slightly different from the next person's, even though that person is also honorable and full of integrity.

Lying, cheating, and stealing might seem like easy ethical issues to deal with, but if someone who's been dieting strenuously asks if the 14 pounds she's lost shows, and you see no difference, do you just say so? A person with one or two tactful pads, those extra little puffs on the inside tips of the fingers, would figure out a way to answer without hurting the other person's feelings.

If a person is a religious zealot, the arch between the thumb and index finger is usually tight, indicating a judgmental attitude. Someone who cherishes spiritual diversity probably wouldn't become best buddies with a zealot. A more religiously diversified person is more likely to have the opposite marking: a wide arch between the thumb and index finger.

Laughing at the same things

Shared laughter keeps friendships going strong. But what is funny to one person might not be funny to another. People with different tastes in humor usually don't make good friends. If raunchiness makes you laugh, chances are the mounts of Luna and Venus are well developed, since they indicate good energy and sexual interest.

A wide arch between the index finger and the thumb could signify people who like raunchy, plus gallows humor, because the arch is a sign of being nonjudgmental.

A pure humorous nature to begin with is shown when the upper portion of the percussion side of the hand has a slight bulge. Look at the hands of comedian Robin Williams, Mexican president Vincente Fox, or television host Rosie O'Donnell for examples. Including President Fox in this list shows that one need not be a noted comedian to have a great sense of humor.

An exceptionally long and thick middle finger can indicate melancholia or depression, so it's not a good indicator of a humorous nature.

Trustworthiness

People naturally want trustworthy friends. Say a secret is shared and the other person tells others about it. If it's intimate, such as someone telling another about contracting herpes, there might be good cause to reconsider the friendship. If the friend shared with others that the person had confided that he or she was contemplating suicide, telling someone who could help seems like the thing for a friend to do.

We carry different expectations in friendships, but a certain amount of trustworthiness can be expected. An uppermost joint of the fingers that is larger than the mid-joint (knuckle) indicates someone who is a meddler and often a gossip—which might be okay under some circumstances, such as on the hands of a gossip columnist, but it's pretty tricky for close friendships. Some people show only developed mid-joints, giving a waist-like appearance to the fingers, but that just means they are more detail-oriented, as opposed to their counterparts with smooth-jointed fingers. This would cause no conflict between friends, and one might balance the other.

We know most little kids are honest, but we're not too sure about people we deal with in business, and we're certain (sometimes) that most politicians and attorneys are dishonest. We rely on friendships and our families to offer a place where we can trustingly bare our souls.

Honesty allows good friends to let down their guards. We don't need to be "up" all the time or carry on a conversation if we don't want to. For women, makeup isn't necessary, and it makes no difference if the gray shows through in our hair.

But in the outside world, away from close friends and family, we might note that a person given to lying, rather than just softening a harsh truth, might have a crooked little finger. Because that is the finger of communication, its crookedness shows the proclivity to bend the truth more than just a little.

Or we might notice the way people hold their hands. When the thumbs are tucked into a fist, it means they're holding something back; hands placed inside pockets may be trying to conceal something, or to show caution in revealing too much.

Listening ability

Friendships involve listening and really hearing what the other person is saying. We're tuned in to our friends. Ironically, noted conversationalists are usually expert listeners. When people leave the company of good conversationalists, they usually feel they had a great time and learned a lot. They're not even aware that good conversationalists listen to and respond to every word the other person says. They aren't the types to just listen while waiting for an opportunity to inject their own opinions. Friends can have differing opinions, but they listen to one another.

Good listeners (good conversationalists) often have long little fingers rather than short ones, as might be expected, because short fingers of Mercury denote a shy person. Shy people may not be too good at making conversation, even though they can listen well. This is simply because good conversation requires a certain amount of participation and even asking questions.

People with longer index fingers might also be good listeners, because leadership ability is often linked with the ability to hear what others are saying.

Arching thumbs that bend back at the top joint belong on the hands of gregarious people who make friends easily and instantly, but those friends are not always long-term friends. These people can be good conversationalists.

Sensitivity

Sensitivity to others is shown by the tactful pads on the inside portion of the fingertips; by thinness in the middle portion of the palm (the great triangle), measured between the inside and outside of the palm; and by markings such as the Ring of Solomon, healer's marks, or St. Andres's Cross. (See Chapter 8.)

The Ring of Solomon, that small ring or line beneath the finger of Jupiter, frequently shows up on the hands of adepts who instinctively know and understand the person they are with; healer's marks, short vertical lines beneath the finger of Mercury leaning toward Apollo, belong on the hands of nurses and others who are deeply concerned with the welfare of others; and St. Andres's Cross, a small line or cross lying between the lines of fate and life, is found on the hands of those who give aid to others and who are often concerned with universal peace.

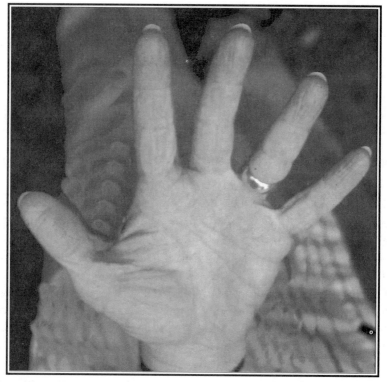

Graphic #53.

Graphics #53 and #54. *The two hands shown here belong to women who have been friends for 30-plus years. The most notable characteristic is that the lines of head and life are separated on both of their hands, showing them to be risk-takers in their beliefs and attitudes. They also have long little fingers, making them good conversationalists, and each has the thumb bump, which means they are avid readers and deep thinkers. The thumbs bend easily into wide arches, indicating that they move easily around groups of people. It's no wonder they make good friends: They share the same political philosophies (and have worked on various campaigns together); are outspoken; are moms of at least four children each; are liberal feminists; and entertain frequently.*

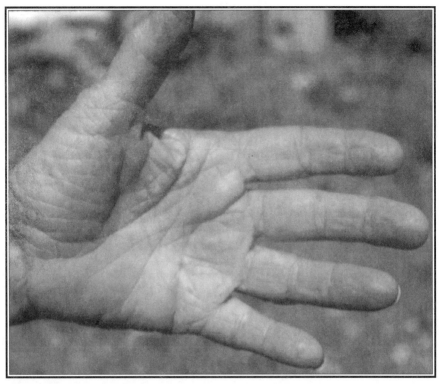

Graphic #54.

Open-mindedness

People who are called "protein people" are those people who are able to blend into any type of group and feel comfortable. They are naturally open-minded and often prefer interacting with others who don't necessarily think, dress, act, or behave as they do. They also are at ease with people from different ethnic groups, socioeconomic backgrounds, educational levels, and sexual orientations.

People who aren't considered "protein" in their outlook on life establish lasting friendships just as easily, but they usually make them with people who are more like themselves.

The hand characteristics that might signal more openness to explore new things are the same ones that provide at least a few of the protein person's characteristics.

A line of head that is separated from the line of life makes one more of a risk-taker and can be a quality of the protein person. A wide arch between the thumb of index finger indicates someone who is open-minded and accepting; and a strong, healthy-looking line of heart free from drooping hair lines can also be an indication, because it portends a healthy and trusting outlook toward others.

The quadrangle, the smooth, flat area between lines of head and heart, indicates a nonjudgmental, broad-minded, and accepting individual. The narrower it becomes, the more bigoted and judgmental the person.

Reliability and loyalty

We like to think that we can count on our friends, and we let our friends know that they can count on us through thick and thin. Maybe a friendship that withers when times get tough (unless people who are down ask too much) wasn't the strongest to begin with.

People who ask too much (such as money for drugs or alcohol or for us to lie for them) are not really close friends. But we do want to believe that when we hit troubled water and the friend has a rowboat, he or she will be there for us.

The hand of a person we're able to count on—in other words, a reliable friend—consists of one or two square-tipped fingers or an Earth/square palm (because Earth/square hands indicate loyalty). This person's hand can also include a balanced quadrangle and/or lines of head and heart that are balanced in depth and color with one another. The latter marking shows that the neither the heart nor head rules, but rather are in balance. One or two of these markings is significant; a hand need not include all of them to indicate reliability and loyalty.

Patience

Patience is required in friendship. It takes a long time to establish a lasting friendship. Those whose thumbs show a longer second phalange than the upper portion (or top) of the thumb, which encompasses the first phalange, tend to have more patience. When that first phalange is the most developed, especially if it is bulbous, it indicates the person with a fiery temper. It may be more difficult for this type of person to establish lasting friendships.

Shares similar interests

Friends, more frequently than not, share some interests, especially when it comes to the working life, although workplace friendships often stay at work, especially after a person leaves for a new job or relocates.

Shared interests in certain sports, church affiliations, political causes, a love of certain music, an interest in education, and membership associations also draw people together.

At least one key factor usually exists, and from that a friendship might begin. Usually other likenesses or agreements will then develop. (See Graphics #53 and #54 on pages 184 and 185.)

Differences on other levels, though, can exist in friendships. Two women (different from the preceding graphics) whose hands I've studied have been friends for more than 30 years. One is an avid hiker and skier; the other doesn't enjoy walking much farther than a trip to the grocery store. But it's interesting to study the likenesses in their hands. They are both interested in the theater and good books. Both have well-developed mounts beneath Apollo, indicating an appreciation for the arts. Neither is biased against any ethnic groups or homosexuals, so a wide space exists between the finger of Jupiter and the thumb, showing them to be nonjudgmental. Both are independent, with wide spaces between the finger of Apollo and Mercury.

Likenesses exist, also, for two men, close friends for more than 40 years, whose hands I've studied. One is a practicing Catholic, and the other has no religious affiliation. One is quiet; the other is boisterous. Both have large families and have been married to their respective wives for more than 40 years, as indicated by their lines of head and life being joined beneath the finger of Jupiter. Both have thumbs that bend back, showing that the men both make friends easily. The arch between the thumb and finger of Jupiter is wide on both hands, indicating tolerance.

CHAPTER 13

LEISURE ACTIVITIES AND

HOBBIES

If a man insisted always on being serious,
and never allowed himself a bit of fun and relaxation,
he would go mad or
become unstable without knowing it.

—Herodotus

Some people are best suited to adventure travel; others are more into exploration of known areas. Some might take up skydiving; others still derive their greatest enjoyment from reading or woodworking. Knowing what we are about to begin with leads us in the right direction. Not everyone is cut out to do volunteer work, and all don't need to take up extreme sports in order to feel fulfilled.

The top leisure activities for Americans aged 18 and beyond age 75, according to a 1997 survey by the U.S. National Endowment for the Arts was exercise.

Other activities included:

▶ Watching sports.

▶ Watching movies.

▶ Trips to amusement parks.

▶ Playing sports.

▶ Working.

▶ Home improvements.

▶ Computer hobbies.

A June 2000 Harris Poll asked one thousand adults to pick their favorite two or three activities. Reading topped that list, followed by television watching and then spending time with family and kids.

Other activities included:

▶ Gardening.

▶ Fishing.

▶ Walking.

▶ Going to the movies.

▶ Computer activities.

▶ Socializing with friends or neighbors.

▶ Exercising.

Mostly what these kinds of surveys point out are the diverse ways we spend our leisure time. Note that in today's culture, leisure is often combined with work and vice versa.

Combining work and play

An example of a sports activity that spills over into work is the karate practiced by Ed Otis, who also teaches the sport at the University of Riverside in California, and who uses martial arts principles in his consulting business, AACT® Training Programs: Awareness, Attitude, Communication, Training.

Graphic #55.

At first glance, the most outstanding characteristic shown in Ed Otis's hand is its strength, which one might expect from an internationally known karate expert. His inside fingertips, however, show tactful pads, which makes him sensitive to the needs of others. His hand is square, with a mixture of fingertip types; this accounts for his ability to not only instruct karate, but to be the first person in the country to teach it at a four-year college. In other words, Ed has not only the discipline and dedication found in the square hand, but also the creativity and adaptability found in the mixed fingertips. He is also a businessman with his own consulting firm, which specializes in mastering conflict/cooperation in the workplace. He uses the psychological and metaphysical principles of karate to achieve his goals. He truly combines his love of karate with his work.

Characteristics of leisure activities

Not all of us can—or want to—be karate experts, but we might be surprised at some of the characteristics on the hands that predispose people to seek certain types of leisure activities.

Palms

People with Earth/square and Fire/spatulate palms will be more likely to take part in activities that involve the use of their bodies. They are more geared to strenuous physical activity than people with Water/conic hands. Air/philosophic palms are in the middle but can be quite physically active if they have square or spatulate fingertips. When the Earth or Fire hands also have square or spatulate-tipped fingers, the motivation for physical exercise as part of their leisure activates will be even greater. They're mountain climbers, backpackers, and adventure travelers.

But don't write off Water/conic hands as laziness personified. Depending on other markings, people with these hands can be just as physically active as anyone else. Exercise just might not be a priority, and the leisure activities may lie in less physically active areas.

Reading, playing a musical instrument, working puzzles, and even playing games on the computer can also be classified as leisure activities. Such activities stimulate the brain (especially in the elderly), and the brain needs stimulation just as much as the body. However, one augments the other: Physical exercise stimulates the brain, and an active brain helps the body to stay in good shape.

The trick may be, as some experts believe, to imbue the exercise with pleasure.

Fingers and thumbs

Those with Air/philosophic or Water/conic hands, and also square- or spatulate-tipped fingers, will be more likely to seek physical activities than if they have pointed fingertips.

Someone who likes getting away from commonly traveled places might sport a little finger that is widely separated from the ring finger, as this shows independence. It could also involve a long finger of Jupiter, which is the sign of people with leadership abilities who might prefer to strike out on their own, rather than joining a travel group.

Individuals with straight thumbs (ones that don't arch backward much) might also be less likely to want to travel in tour groups, because they don't require people around them all the time. People who have arching thumbs are people persons. They have no trouble at all striking up a friendly conversation, and they might prefer a tour group over going it on their own. They're also more likely to enjoy travel cruises. Tour directors more than likely possess arching thumbs.

Those with long fingers of Apollo (nearly as much as or longer than the finger of Jupiter) might like their vacations near a casino or two, because a long Apollo finger is a sign of a gambler.

Mounts

People with well-developed mounts, especially beneath the finger of Apollo, would be more likely to travel to Europe to take in the museums and art galleries than just to "see Europe," because they have an inherent appreciation of the arts.

A palm that puffs out in the lower portion on the percussion side of the hand between the front and back of the hand usually indicates people who enjoy water sports.

A raised mount beneath the finger of Saturn belongs to someone who enjoys classical music.

Lines of head and life

The need to push the body to its limits will be even more pronounced if the lines of head and life are widely separated beneath the finger of Jupiter. (See Graphic #56.) The wide separation represents someone who is a risk-taker. The wider it is, the more likely the person takes risks with his or her body. A narrow separation indicates risk-taking with the mind and in business.

Line of life

A line of life that ends in a fork just up from the wrist indicates a restless nature, and one that likes to see new things, and experience the offbeat. In addition to a love of travel, these people often enjoy moving to new locations. Their interests may be eclectic, veering from bicycling to reading.

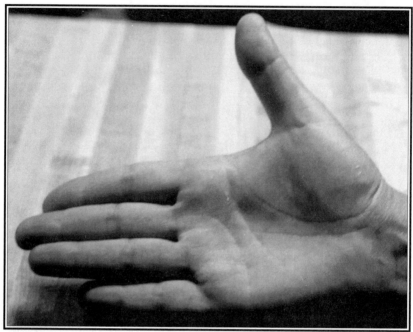

Graphic #56. An Air/philosophic hand.

This hand depicts separated lines of head and life, which makes this man a risk-taker in business and intellectually. His square-tipped fingers supply him with plenty of energy, so he's far from being a couch potato. A dentist who runs his own business, he's also a hunter who travels to remote areas to hike and spend time by himself. He's been known to just shoot the camera instead of his gun, and he finds himself doing more photo shoots the older he gets. He remains adamant about the right of gun ownership and has given talks to organizations such as the Sierra Club on the reasons for those rights. His approach is gentle and persuasive, which goes along with the philosophic bent of his hand. His little finger is quite short, so it's not easy for him to speak in front of groups. Note his thumb, too, with its exceptionally long second phalange, indicating that logic rules his thinking. Also note the well-defined lines of fate and life, indicating a person who makes a life plan and tries to follow it through. He expects a great deal from himself and becomes disappointed when things don't go smoothly as planned. The line of heart heading between Jupiter and Saturn indicates that he also expects a great deal from a mate.

Travel lines

Not all travelers will produce travel lines, but look back at Graphic #48 in Chapter 10 (the pilot's hand) to see several small horizontal lines at the bottom of Luna just up from the wrist bracelets. As a helicopter pilot who now owns his own real estate business, as well as a plane, this man has literally traveled and worked throughout the world.

Then look at Graphic #15 in Chapter 3 for a well-traveled woman who, nevertheless, has no travel lines. She traveled to various parts of the world throughout her life, preferring the less-traveled road with some adventure, as shown by the separated lines of life and head. She was an avid backpacker, owned a bookstore, and became a full-time deputy sheriff in her 40s, shortly before her untimely death of a brain tumor.

Travel lines

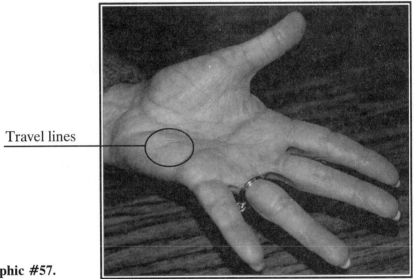

Graphic #57.

This is the hand of a woman who has made travel part of her life. Note the horizontal travel lines in the upper portion of the mount of Luna. The mounts are well developed, indicating that she likes to see it all when traveling and would push on even if she had a broken foot. She wants to take advantage of every minute. Her hand is Air with some square-tipped fingers, which makes her less likely to want adventure travel, but she still has the drive to "see and taste it all." She's a Los Angeles–area schoolteacher who lived and taught in a variety of countries before returning to the United States, but her wanderlust never left.

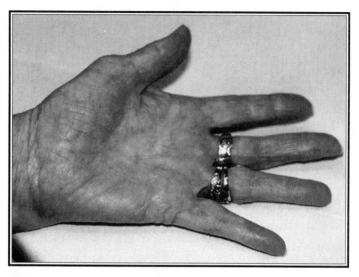

Graphic #58.

The travel lines on author Marilyn Meredith's hand can be seen at the bottom of her hand, running from the percussion side of the palm upwards toward the center of the palm.

The variety of leisure activities available today can just about fulfill anyone's needs, which are different based on an individual's type of personality. It's okay to like or not like cruises; to prefer guided tours or not; to desire a trip that produces something, such as an archeological dig, or to want a vacation of just lying around on a white sandy beach.

Leisure activities can also include trips or sports related to work and involve pursuits close to home that involve little travel. Some of these likes and dislikes show in the hand, which provides a license to pursue them.

 AND GESTURES

Some people can't talk without waving around their arms about, but gesturing with the hands may be what fires the brain. Linguists, psychologists who study body language and speech, anthropologists, and other communication experts estimate that humans use more than three thousand hand gestures. Studies show that hand gestures are an integral part of communication, both for the speaker and listener, and that language may have arisen from hand gestures. Also, words make up only 7 percent of communication, whereas body language (chiefly hand gestures) makes up the bulk of communication.

When people aren't allowed to gesture, it interferes with the communication and thought processes. Two blind people talking together use hand gestures, and many people use them when talking on the telephone, even though their listener can't see them, according to Jana Iverson, assistant professor of psychology at the University of Missouri-Columbia.

Based on chimpanzee studies, some researchers believe that hand gestures may once have been the only means of communication by humans. Also, when certain areas of the brain controlling language are damaged, so are the normal gestures that go with talking.

Simply observing the way people hold their hands and fingers tells us a great deal about them. Some of the positions, however, can be temporary, such as when speaking to a group of people.

At other times we can be filled with energy or dragging, we may want to conceal something for our own protection, or we may be feeling on top of the world. These feelings are all reflected in our hands.

Although all cultures have certain gestures that are similar in meaning to one another, many have different connotations.

Many gestures used today are based in antiquity, such as the "fig hand," with the fingers slightly curled inward toward the palm and the thumb tucked in the center.

Depictions of hands in various forms have been used since ancient times to ward off the "evil eye" and other ill omens. One of these is the thumb and first two fingers extended with the ring and little finger curled in toward the palm. Such a position is still used today by some Christian churches during the Benedictine.

General hand and finger movements

Some hand gestures that are common to Americans take on special meaning after being used and observed by large numbers of people. For example:

▶ A hand punched into the air is a sign of victory or an exceptionally good feeling about something.

▶ Rubbing one's hands can be a sign of joy.

▶ Placed on a table, hands that are wider apart than the person's shoulders show an aggressive nature. If they're about equal to the shoulders, the person is balanced in his or her approach. Hands close together on the table mean the person is being cautious.

▶ If the hands touch when laid out flat on a table, the individual plans to take a conservative approach.

▶ When the hands are flat on the table with no arch, people mean business. A slight arch means they might give a little, because they are less sure of themselves.

▶ Wringing the hands, or grasping the top side of the head with a hand, is a sign of despair.

▶ A bent little finger (inward toward the palm, not to a side) is indicative of a sense of failure and impotence.

▸ Hands hanging limply at a person's side indicate indecision; a clenched fist by the side means strong will and determination.

▸ Arms folded across the chest with the hands tucked inside show someone who doubts what the other person is saying.

▸ A gently clenched fist can stand for determination; a tightly clenched fist can show frustration and anger.

▸ A tightly clenched fist with the thumb tucked beneath the curled fingers is the sign of the miser—not only with money, but also in personal relationships.

▸ Hands clasped together with the fingers entwined indicate individuals who are contemplating a move.

▸ Hands placed together without the fingers entwined, but with the thumbs wrapped around each other, indicate that the person is waiting for the other person to make a move.

▸ An index finger touching tip of the nose can indicate someone trying to make up his or her mind.

▸ A clenched hand with the thumb or a finger pressed against the lips means the person is contemplating his or her next move.

▸ Hands held behind the back indicate those who aren't quite sure of a situation and who are waiting to make a decision.

▸ Apollo and Mercury bent inward indicates someone who's afraid to speak his or her mind at the time or is unwilling to face the truth of something. If only Apollo curves in, the person is withholding information.

▸ Fingers held straight show self-confidence.

▸ Covering the face with the hands can be a sign of embarrassment, sadness, or shame.

Cultural hand gesture differences

Not all gestures are limited in use to one particular culture. Many gestures take on different meanings depending on the culture in which they're used. Here are some examples:

▶ In Japan, a thumb pointed in the air means "my boss"; in the United States, the thumb's up means "good" or "well done." In some Islamic countries, it's equivalent to giving the bird. In Australia, it's considered rude. In Bangladesh, it is a taunt.

▶ A circle made with the thumb and index finger means "okay" in the United States but stands for "money" or "zero" in Japan.

▶ The United States' shame-on-you sign (rubbing one index finger over the other) means two angry or fighting individuals in Japan.

▶ Circling the index finger near the ear, a common sign Americans give to someone whom they deem as talking or acting "crazy" is the same in Japan, but the Japanese mean really crazy. In Argentina, the same sign tells a person he or she has a telephone call.

▶ Tapping the middle of the forehead in Holland means the person is crazy.

▶ In Europe, waving hello and goodbye involves the palm facing outward, the hand and arm stationary, and the fingers moving up and down. American wave side to side. A side-to-side wave in Greece means "no."

▶ In many countries, the American hitchhiking thumb is considered rude.

▶ Finger-snapping is considered vulgar in France or Belgium.

▶ Americans cross their fingers for luck, but in Paraguay it is offensive.

▶ Pointing the index finger is offensive in Middle Eastern countries. It is also considered bad taste in the United States, especially when it's pointed at a person.

▶ It's a curse in parts of Africa for the little finger and index finger to be raised with the two middle fingers down. To some Hawaiians it means "hang loose," and to some Italians it means a person's wife is unfaithful.

▶ Palms and fingertips up in the United States can mean "stop," but in Greece it can signal a confrontation. In some parts of Africa, it's the same as giving the bird.

▶ What is called "steepling" of the fingers, used by physicians and psychiatrists who touch the fingers of both hands together as in deep thought, is perceived by those in the Western world as a sign of intelligence.

Speech experts tell us to keep our hands out in the open and to use them. Would we really trust a politician who kept his hands behind his back? That's because our hand movements are an integral part of how we're feeling and what we're thinking.

Hand meditation

The venerable Luangpor Teean Jittasubho (1911–1988), a Buddhist monk, is responsible for developing a meditation practice with the hands that can be used while sitting, standing, or lying down. He believed that "mindfulness" such as concentrating on the hand movements (he also encouraged walking mindfulness) led to awareness that would help us see the clear, pure freedom of life. He developed a routine of simple movements to clear the mind. I do them to relieve stress sitting at the computer for long hours. The idea is to "think" about nothing but the movements. Here they are:

1. Place both hands on the thighs, palm down.

2. Mindfully turn the right hand sideways and stop.

3. Mindfully raise the right hand and forearm and stop.

4. Mindfully lower the right hand to rest on the abdomen and stop.

5. Mindfully turn the left hand sideways and stop.

6. Mindfully raise the left hand and forearm and stop.

7. Mindfully lower the left hand to rest on top of the right hand on the abdomen.

8. Mindfully slide the right hand to the chest and stop.

9. Mindfully move the right hand outward and stop.

10. Mindfully lower the right hand, touch the right thigh, and stop.

11. Mindfully turn the right palm down on the thigh.

12. Mindfully slide the left hand to the chest and stop.

13. Mindfully move the left hand outward and stop.

14. Mindfully lower the left hand, touch the left thigh, and stop.

15. Mindfully turn the palm of the left hand down on the thigh.

TIME LINES

In order to determine the age at which an event is likely to occur, several measurements are possible individually and overlaid with one another. It is not exacting, and three or four years on either side of the determined date can be considered. The more hands a person reads, the better able he or she can tell dates of certain events in a person's life.

Line of life time lines

Approximate years on the line of life are read from the beginning of the line to its end, as illustrated in Graphic #59.

Line of fate time lines reading up

Approximate years as shown on the line of fate reading from the wrist upward, as illustrated in Graphic #60.

Line of fate time lines reading down

Approximate years as shown on the line of fate reading down from near the center of the palm, as illustrated in Graphic #61. When the line of fate doesn't begin until mid-life or later, it can be read down (rather than up from the wrist) from about the center of the palm and ending toward the wrist. This descending line can often be seen on the hands of women who have raised their children and then decided to join the workforce.

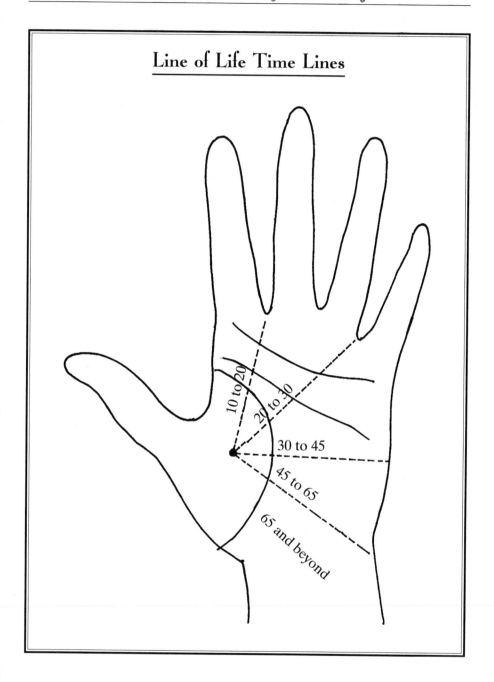

Graphic #59. Line of Life Time Lines.

Line of FateTime Line

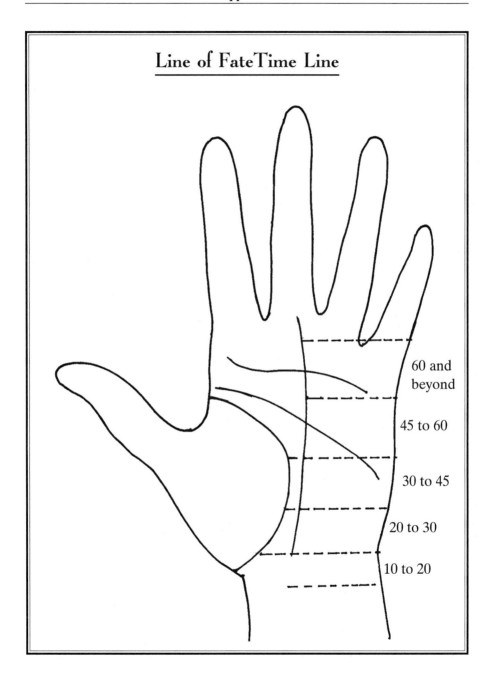

60 and beyond

45 to 60

30 to 45

20 to 30

10 to 20

Graphic #60. Line of Fate Time Lines Reading Up.

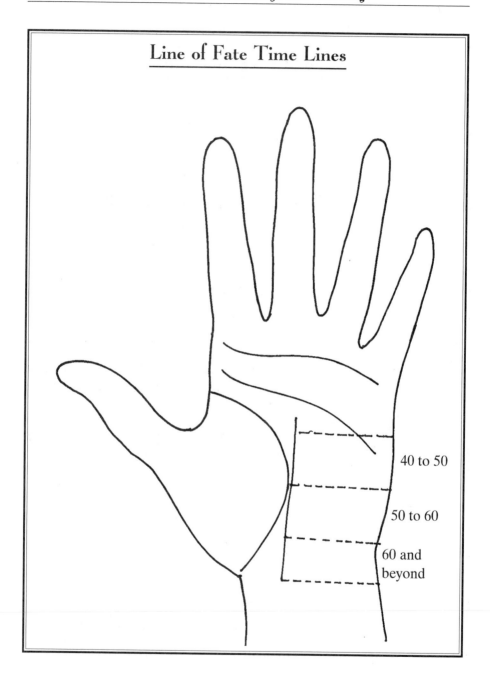

Line of Fate Time Lines

40 to 50

50 to 60

60 and beyond

Graphic #61. Line of Fate Time Lines Reading Down.

# GLOSSARY

A

Affection lines: Small horizontal lines running beneath the little finger and above the line of heart on the percussion side of the hand. Also called love, relationship, or marriage lines.

Air hand: The astrological designation referring to elongated shape of the palm. Fingers are usually also long.

Allergy line: A horizontal line running along the base of the mount of Luna near the wrist bracelets.

Ambidextrous: Having the ability to use either hand equally well or to use either for performing certain tasks.

Antibody or Mars line: A small line or lines running parallel to and inside the line of life that stem from the lower Mars mount.

Apollo: The name of the ring finger and of the mount beneath it. Also the Roman sun god. The line running toward that finger from anywhere on the hand is called a line of Apollo.

Arch: The ability of fingers or thumb to curve backward from the palm.

Attendant line: Lines that run parallel to another line, adding strength to the major line. Sometimes called sister or backup lines, which run parallel to a prime line.

Avoidance line: A short horizontal line at the bottom of the line of life, which may or may not touch the line of life. Also referred to as the escape line.

Birth hand: The non-dominant hand.

Capillary lines: Faint lines drooping from major or minor lines that sap energy.

Cephalic line: A small line running next to the line of health. Also known as the Via Lasciva.

Chains: Oval or circular chain-like formations that appear on some lines.

Children lines: Short vertical lines running upwards from the marriage or relationship lines.

Circles: Small markings usually found on lines or mounts.

Clubbed thumb tips: Tips shaped like clubs or light bulbs.

Conic: A hand shape with tapered, pointed fingertips or a slightly elongated shaped palm. Also referred to as a Water hand.

Cross: A stand-alone cross with a separate meaning from major or minor lines that cross one another.

Cross bars: Groups of independent crossed lines. Also referred to as grills or grids. Can sometimes be signs of misfortune, except on the mounts of Jupiter or Luna.

Curiosity line: A short horizontal line on the mount of Jupiter near the side of the hand.

Dermal ridges: Upper layers of the epidermis (skin) that form the fingerprints.

Developed mounts: Puffy or raised areas of the palm generally found beneath the fingers, the thumb, and the percussion side of the hand.

Dominant hand: The preferred hand.

Dots: Tiny, solid circles found independently on the palm or the lines on the palm.

Earth hand: The astrological designation referring to a square-shaped palm.

Earth mount: A spongy, sometimes hard mount on the outside of the hand by the bottom portion of the thumb. It can be found by pressing the thumb against the side of the hand beneath Jupiter.

Elastic: Firm, yet pliable skin or mounts.

Escape line: A short horizontal line at the bottom of the line of life, which may or may not touch the line of life. Also called the avoidance line.

Fingerprints: Dermal ridges on the tips of the fingers.

Fire hand: The astrological designation referring to a palm that is wider at the bottom or top and that narrows at the opposite end of the palm. Also referred to as spatulate-shaped.

Firm-jointed: Fingers or thumbs with minimal backward bend or arch.

Flexible: Arching back toward the back of the hand.

Flexion creases: Scientists' name for the major lines in the hand. Also referred to as palmar creases.

Forked lines: Extra lines at the beginning or endings of lines that usually add strength.

Friendship lines: Horizontal lines on the mount of Venus that do not touch the line of life.

Gene: A physical unit that carries characteristics from parent to child.

Genetic: The means by which traits are passed from parent to offspring.

Gestation: The period of fertilization from an egg to birth.

Girdle of Venus: A horizontal line running above the line of life.

Great triangle: The area that usually encompasses the narrowest and center portion of the palm between the line of life and line of head. Its narrowest point is beneath the finger of Jupiter, and its widest area opens toward the mount of Luna.

Grills: Cross-hatched lines sometimes meaning misfortune, except on the mounts of Jupiter or Luna.

Handedness: The propensity toward use of either right or left hands.

Handshake: The grasping of another's hand and usually pumping it up or down.

Healer's marks: Short vertical lines on the mount of Mercury.

High-set thumbs: Thumbs that stem from about the middle of the mount of Venus.

Indulgence line: A small, slanting line on the wrist at the bottom of mount of Luna indicating a propensity for self-indulgence.

Inheritance lines: Lines appearing in the arch between the fingers of Mercury and Apollo and traveling downward toward the line of heart.

Jupiter: Chief Roman god or deity used in naming the index finger and the mount beneath it.

Knot: A bulge in joints of fingers.

Knotty-jointed: Having developed joints that make the phalanges look waist-shaped or thin.

Knuckles: The third joints, which are nearest to the palm.

Ladders: Small bunches of lines that cross main lines.

Left hand: Usually the non-dominant hand.

Line of Apollo: The line on the palm running toward the mount of Apollo.

Line of fate: The horizontal line usually stemming from the middle of the palm and running upwards. Can also stem from other areas on the palm.

Line of head: The major horizontal line on the palm referring to the intellect.

Line of health: The line that runs vertical from the direction of the finger of Mercury. Sometimes referred to as Hepatica.

Line of heart: The major horizontal line on the palm referring to a person's love or friendship capabilities.

Line of life: The major line on the palm referring to a person's potential for quality of life.

Line of stubbornness: The line located on the thumb near the bottom of the second joint.

Love lines: Lines found on the percussion side of the palm at its outer edge between the little finger and the line of heart. Also referred to as relationship, marriage, or affection lines.

Lower Mars mount: The area found inside the line of life in the lower portion of the arch between the thumb and the finger of Jupiter. Its name derives from the Roman war god.

Low-set thumbs: Thumbs that begin fairly close to the wrist and usually appear shorter than high-set thumbs (although they may not actually be shorter when measured).

Luna mount: The area found on the lower portion of the palm on the percussion side of the hand. The Latin name for the moon goddess, Selene. Also referred to as Artemis or Diana in different mythological references.

Major lines: The lines of life, head, and heart. Called palmar or flexion creases by scientists.

Marriage lines: Lines found on the percussion side of the palm at its outer edge between the little finger and the line of heart. Also referred to as relationship, love, or affection lines.

Mars: Roman war god.

Mars (lower mount): A mount that signifies a high or low pain tolerance.

Mars (upper mount): A mount that signifies assertiveness and resiliency.

Mercury: The name of the little finger and of the mount beneath it. Also the Roman messenger of the gods.

Moon line: A small line on the mount of Luna curving into the palm. Sometimes called the line of intuition.

Mounts: Raised portions on the palm generally most noticeable beneath the fingers, surrounding the thumb, and on the percussion side of the hand. Smaller, less important mounts also appear on some hands.

Mount of Apollo: The mount found beneath the ring finger on the palm.

Mount of Jupiter: The mount found beneath the index finger on the palm.

Mount of Luna: The mount found on the percussion side of the hand opposite the mount of Venus.

Mount of Mercury: The mount found beneath the little finger on the palm.

Mount of Neptune: The mount located just above the wrist bracelets on the palm between Venus and Luna.

Mount of Pluto: The mount located on the lower part of the palm near the wrist bracelets on the percussion side of the hand.

Mount of Saturn: The mount found beneath the middle finger on the palm.

Mount of Venus: The mount that surrounds the thumb on the palm inside the line of life.

Non-dominant hand: The hand not naturally favored for use by the person. Referred to as the birth hand in palm reading.

Old Soul mount: The large raised area that lies practically beneath the wrist bracelets on the percussion side of the hand.

Palmar creases: The major lines of the hand. Also called flexion creases.

Percussion: The little finger side of the hand.

Phalanges: The three sections of the fingers between the joints and between the two parts of the thumb.

Philosophic: A hand with a tapering, full shape. Also referred to as Air hand.

Philosopher's bump: A bump found at the bottom of the thumb that indicates an inquiring nature, usually a reader with philosophic tendencies. Also called the thumb bump.

Quadrants: The four sections or categories of the palm.

Quadrangle: The flat space between the lines of head and heart that determines a stable personality.

Relationship lines: Lines found on the percussion side of the palm at its outer edge between the little finger and the line of heart. Also referred to as marriage, love, or affection lines.

Right hand: Usually the dominant hand.

Ring of Saturn: A small horizontal line or ring found beneath the Saturn finger.

Ring of Solomon: A small line beneath the finger of Jupiter. Sometimes referred to as the Ring of Jupiter.

Saturn: The name of the middle finger and of the mount beneath it. Also the Roman god of agriculture.

Simian line: The lines of head and heart combined and running horizontally across the palm. Also referred to as the Sydney line.

Skin texture: The thickness of skin involving depth and breadth of skin ridges.

Smooth: Fingers without protruding joints.

Spatulate: A hand shaped like a spatula—that is, being either broader at the top or the bottom and tapering in the opposite direction. Also referred to as the Fire hand; fingertips that flare and that are shaped like a spatula.

Spots: Tiny dots found on lines or mounts.

Squares: Small markings that usually surround a break in a line, island, circle, spot, or ladder.

Square: A hand with a palm that's nearly equal in breadth and length and sturdy looking. Also referred to as an Earth hand.

Square: Fingers that are squared off at the tip.

St. Andres's Cross: A lateral line near the wrist between the lines of health and fate.

Stiff fingers or thumb: The opposite of the supple, or arching, thumb or fingers.

Sydney line: The lines of head and heart combined and running horizontally across the palm. Also referred to as the Simian line.

Tactful pads: Extra little pads on the inside tips of the fingers.

Tasseled lines: Lines that end or begin with tassels.

Temper line: The line found directly above the second (or lowest) joint on the thumb.

Thumb bump: A bump found on the lowest joint of the thumb. Also called the philosopher's bump.

Travel lines: Short little lines on the mount of Luna between the line of fate and the percussion side of the hand. Travel lines can also arise from the wrist bracelets.

Upper Mars mount: The mount found beneath the little finger just below the line of heart. Its name derives from the Roman war god.

Via Lasciva: A small line running next to the line of health. Also called the cephalic line.

Volar pads: Dermal ridges; fingerprints.

Venus: A major mount on the thumb side of the palm. Also known as Aphrodite, the Roman and Greek goddess of love and beauty.

Water hand: The astrological designation referring to a tapered, well-padded hand shape and tapering, pointed fingers.

Wrist bracelets: Horizontal lines that cut across the wrist just below the palm. Also referred to as rascettes.

Waist-shaped: Fingers that have full, or protruding joints, making the phalanges look waist-shaped or narrow.

INDEX

BOUT THE AUTHOR

Rita Robinson is a former reporter and award-winning journalist with specialities in health and psychology. In addition to more than 1,000 published magazine articles and 10 books to her credit, she has studied palm reading for 35 years and has written three books on the subject. She has appeared on radio and TV in connection with several of her books, including those on palmistry, and also conducts writing workshops at several colleges and writing conferences. She can be contacted via e-mail at ritarobn@gte.net or through her palmistry Web site at *www.handscape.com*.